A Way of Life
Less Common

Modern Day Pioneers
Volume One

A Way of Life Less Common
Modern Day Pioneers
Volume One

Published by Cottage Country Press
ISBN 978-0-9866460-3-4
Edited by Christine Dixon
Proofread by Kianna Walpole
Front cover photo (Sauble River) courtesy of Mike Carter
Interior design & layout by Christine Dixon
Cover design by Christine Dixon & Mike Carter

This book is dedicated to all those who contributed to
A Way of Life Less Common
Modern Day Pioneers
Volume One

For without you, this book would not have been possible...

A Way of Life Less Common

Table of Contents

A Way of Life Less Common

Preface

W hat began as a research project to learn more about living in the bush, going off-grid, and homesteading quickly evolved into this first volume of *A Way of Life Less Common*.

My initial goal was to learn from others who had done what my partner Mike and I intended to do. As I began reading and learning about the experiences of others, I quickly realized that there were likely many people, like us, also contemplating this lifestyle, who would also benefit from learning more about these remarkable people and their experiences.

This was the beginning of the rewarding experience of contacting the people I'd been reading about, interviewing each of them, and then creating this book.

What evolved was this first volume, a collection of interviews with very fascinating people who have already achieved our dream. These pioneers of the new frontier have all left their old ways of life to embark on an adventure, a change, and most of all, a way of life less common.

Some are completely off-grid, while others have chosen to keep some of the old conveniences—but *all* have learned to be more self-sufficient.

From Washington to Colorado, Northern Ontario to British Columbia, these people are enjoying life away from the busy cities, surrounded by nature and reaping the benefits of their hard work and determination.

For many of those interviewed, earning a living is still very much a part of their lives, and they have shared this information as well—proof that it can be done.

It was such an honour to get to know the people that you will meet on the following pages. They were all willing to share insights into the process, their motivations, triumphs and pitfalls, as well as their feelings about their decisions.

I'd like to thank each of the participants for their time, their willingness to share, their photos, and for the honour of allowing us to glimpse into their worlds.

I truly hope that these interviews inspire, teach and motivate you as much as they have done for Mike and me. There truly is an enriching, fulfilling life awaiting those who are prepared for the challenges and rewards of leaving the rat race behind and embarking on *A Way of Life Less Common.*

A Way of Life

Less Common

Modern Day Pioneers

Good Ideas for Life

Laurie & Ed Essex

Laurie and Ed live on 40 acres in eastern Washington, surrounded by pine, fir and tamarack trees, right next door to a national forest.

Good Ideas for Life

*L*aurie and Ed got together in 2004. At the time, Laurie had just left a job running a horse farm in Colorado, and Ed was starting a business in commercial masonry construction.

They had actually met in Sunday school when he was six and she was five years old. They even went to middle and high school together. Apparently interests changed over time because as Ed lovingly admitted—they liked each other a lot more in their 50's than they did in the early years.

They were living in a condominium in the town where they had both grown up when they made the decision to change their lives. Ed already owned a cabin in a recreational development on the Columbia River where they spent as much time as possible enjoying the climate and all the area had to offer.

Making the choice to homestead, live off-grid and/or live in the bush is a life changing decision. What initially led you to make this choice?

We were approached by a realtor to sell our cabin and decided to put it on the market at a fairly high price and see what might happen. Three weeks later we were offered our asking price and sold it—just like that! Now what were we going to do?

I had family friends living even further east so we went to visit them. We fell in love with the whole area and started looking for property right away. It took us a year to find what we were looking for and made an offer which was accepted.

Laurie had always wanted to live on the east side of the state. It rains a lot on the west side but you do have a lot of forests, lakes, rivers and the Puget Sound. The eastern side of the state is more arid and in Laurie's case, more suitable for horses, which she wanted to get back into. I had been making trips to eastern Washington for most of my adult life to pursue outdoor interests.

Our property is located in beautiful pine forests and natural pasture right next to National Forest land. It had everything we wanted. We thought we could use it to camp on for a few years and then *maybe* build our retirement home when the time came.

That time came sooner than expected. When the not-so-great recession hit, my business didn't slow down—it ended. There were no more jobs in my line of work. None.

We had to make a change.

I had been doing research for three years on living off-grid and had a basic home design. We decided to get serious about it, and the rest is history.

We had to go off-grid by necessity because there were no amenities where we were moving to. The idea of being independent and a little more sustainable appealed to us both. Solar was becoming more common, practical and affordable.

Prior to making this decision, were you already familiar with this lifestyle? Were you outdoor-lovers? Farmers or gardeners? Hunters? Working at home? Campers?

When I was a kid I was always outside and so was Laurie. When I got older I hunted, camped, fished, skied, and became a certified diver.

Laurie also spent all of her time outdoors on horseback or sailing and camping in the San Juan Islands. She is well traveled—both worldwide and in the US.

We both commercially fished as well. That's how Laurie put herself through college.

I heated my home for years with wood that I cut and split myself.

What were your biggest concerns, fears or other factors that you had to consider?

Laurie didn't have any, but I did. How would we make a living? Running our own ecommerce business from home sounded good—but would we be successful? Could we really do the things we thought we could from research alone? Was I willing to leave a place I had spent my whole life? Also, I was worried about leaving the area, when my parents were getting up in age.

How long was it, from the time you made the decision to the time you actually made the move, and why?

Literally as long as it took to close my business, build a new house and start a new company—about two years. We had been talking about it for another year before that—just for fun.

How did your family react? Please include the reactions of immediate family as well as extended family if possible.

Laurie's parents are gone, but she has one son. He has been living on his own for a long time so he wasn't too much of a consideration. He has always been supportive of whatever his mother wanted to do.

My family has also been supportive. Both of my kids are grown and on their own. Since we started this move I lost my dad and it was hard to leave my mother behind at this stage of her life. We both have some regrets about this move but we both understand why I did it.

How did you know that you had found the perfect property?

Our property suits most of our needs, but not all. It is difficult to access. We are three miles off the nearest paved road. We have to maintain the road ourselves. There is no one else to do it. All of the surrounding properties are for recreational use and without any amenities—like power—it isn't likely anyone else will build here. That is also the *good news* about our property.

Not only do we have to maintain our road but I have to keep it plowed in the winter as well.

I don't like it that our property is on a slope but Laurie does because it's good to help the horses keep fit, and it also allows us an incredible view.

We do love our view and the surrounding pine forests here. We also love the general location. We are surrounded by National Forest land. We have 5 lakes within 10 miles, just loaded with fish. We can hunt, hike, camp, fish, ride horses, and even pan for gold just by going down the driveway and entering the National Forest next door.

Were you nervous about your decision, and if so, why?

We weren't sure everything would work the way our research showed. It turns out we were probably 95% accurate. All of our unique systems such as: solar power, concrete house construction, masonry heating, and water cisterns work just the way we planned them to. We even went through a forest fire the first year and all of the precautions we took to make our house fireproof worked fantastic!

I don't think you can totally prepare for this drastic a change in lifestyle and that turned out to be true.

What were your intentions? To go off-grid? Become self-sufficient? Escape the rat race?

Laurie and I wanted to live in a place that was not so crowded with people.

We wanted to be more self-sufficient than our city/condo lifestyle allowed for.

We honestly felt that—in the pursuit of convenience—we had lost our way somewhat. We wanted to adopt some of the older practices, like growing and preserving our own food the way our parents did. We wanted to reduce our environmental impact, not because of global warming or any other political arguments, but because it just makes sense to do so.

Neither of us is an environmentalist or anything extreme concerning the environment, sustainability, nor anything like that. We just think it is common sense to be less wasteful or destructive to our environment. It is common sense to eat healthy foods, breathe cleaner air, and be more active physically—just by living the way we do.

We thought it would be healthier and more beneficial physically, mentally, and spiritually to live a more sustainable, less convenient lifestyle.

Did you buy a property with a home/cabin already in place or did you build? Why did you make that choice?

There was a very small rustic cabin/home on this property when we bought it. It was torn down by hand, hauled away and reused for another house as an addition. Even the insulation was reused.

We had to start fresh in order to accomplish what we wanted on our property. We wanted a fire-proof, earthquake-proof and energy efficient home

We started from scratch with a new home. It was to encompass passive solar design, a 97% efficient heating system, natural heating and cooling, energy efficient appliances, solar power, and be earthquake and fireproof as much as possible.

Has there ever been a time since you made the move that you wished you hadn't? What happened to make you feel this way and how did you deal with these emotions or situations?

Laurie has loved it here unconditionally since day one.

I have had trouble being away from my family, who are all back home where I came from. There are age and health issues many of them are dealing with and I'm not there to help them.

Other than that—I also have no regrets.

Please share information about your property, such as the amount of land you purchased, your surroundings, and type of home that you chose to build, as well as any building features you decided to include.

We own 40 acres, which is roughly ¼ mile x ¼ mile. It is at a 15% slope. It is 40% forested with pine, fir and tamarack. The rest is natural grass and a little bit of sagebrush near the lower portion.

We created a level spot for the house and barn. Our house sits pretty close to the middle of the property.

We built a house out of insulated concrete foam. The living area is 1400 square feet but we also have an attached garage, carport, covered front porch and woodshed—all under one roof. Our roof is huge.

All of the building is made out of non-combustible materials on the outside. We even covered all of the exposed garage, barn lean-to, and front porch ceilings with metal, to be more fire resistant.

How much did your life change on a daily routine basis? Did you go from working in an office in a downtown setting to getting up every morning and gardening/chopping wood/ etc...?

That's exactly what we did. I used to be in my office at 7:00 every morning until 5:00 at night. Now we start chores in the morning and finish at 5:00 pm.

There is a lot to do. We have two websites. One is our ecommerce site and the other is our blog site. I also blog for Mother Earth News E Magazine.

We have 2 horses, 15 chickens, 2 cats and a dog to take care of. We grow vegetables almost all year long. In the winter we use our built-in insulated greenhouse to grow them; in the summer— the garden.

We cut all the wood we use to heat and cook with. I do all of our solar and other equipment maintenance. We have miles of fencing to maintain. We also maintain our three mile long gravel access road.

What appliances and other household items did you choose not to have and why? Which ones did you choose to keep and why?

Living off-grid just naturally requires you to change some of your habits. There is something about producing your own power that necessitates that. It seems to be a completely natural process.

Even if you weren't before, you are going to *want* to save power and water, and waste less of everything in general. It just seems to be a by-product of this lifestyle.

I don't think we gave up anything. We have TV, a computer and a microwave, just like everyone else.

We have a tank-less hot water heater. It has a little generator in the water line that ignites the flame when you turn the water on. We have a propane stove that is very simple. It has a light in the oven and burner igniters, otherwise nothing else electric.

Other than that we have a washer, dryer, vacuum cleaner and any other electric appliance that most households have. We also have an electric refrigerator and chest freezer. We even have a 220 volt water pump.

Solar power is not what it used to be. It has come a long way. We can have all of the electric conveniences we used to have.

We just don't pollute the atmosphere in order to have them.

It's not really about what you have but how you use it. We turn our lights off when done. We limit our water usage. We don't *always* flush the toilet after every single use. We dry our clothes outside most of the time.

What are the most useful items that you use? This could be something like a snowmobile/ATV or even something as simple as a kitchen utensil that makes your life easier/more enjoyable. More than one item is welcome here.

The Polaris!

How do you heat your home, power your home, wash clothes, cook, and obtain water?

We heat our home with a masonry heater. It is the cleanest heat source, known to be over 95% efficient. We have 40 acres of trees that more than offset our negative carbon impact. We actually have a positive carbon imprint on the environment, even after using all of our appliances and utilities.

We grow our own heat source—wood. We burn about five cords per year at an elevation of 4200'.

Power is solar.

We have an electric washer and propane dryer.

We have an electric toaster and all of the other small appliances you would see in anyone's house.

We have an electric dishwasher.

We have a 300' deep well with a 22V electric pump.

We have our own septic system.

We have backup propane wall heaters in case we want to leave the house for an extended period of time.

The only things to avoid by going off the grid are an electric stove and dryer. Everything else can remain the same.

What do you miss from your old life? Please elaborate.

It is harder to be more sufficient. At our age we do miss many of the conveniences of living *on the grid* in town.

We never had to grow our own food, cut our own wood to heat with, maintain a three mile long road, plow the same road for 5 months of the year, butcher chickens and take care of so many animals.

On the other hand, it is fun to watch TV in a fully lit room when the rest of the area is without power. The food is safer and we know the physical requirements of our lifestyle are good for us.

What is the biggest challenge, or challenges that you faced after making the move?

For us it was making a living. All of our research said we could make a decent living online, but it isn't like it used to be. There is more competition now, and at the same time we opened our online store, Google changed all of the search engine rules. It used to be that you could become visible quickly with a few programming tricks and gimmicks, but now you have to grow your business the old-fashioned way—through time and effort. That's okay but we didn't expect it to take so long because it didn't use to.

(Prior to their new life, Ed had 15 years of grocery retail and 28 years commercial construction experience. Laurie has a two year accounting degree, is a licensed massage therapist, and horse trainer with a British Horse Society Instructors Certificate—the highest horse certification you can get.)

How did you provide food for your family? Did you continue to shop at grocery stores/frequent farmer's markets/barter/grow your own? Please specify for both produce and meat/fish.

We catch our own fish. We fish for kokanee which are land-locked sockeye salmon. We call them mountain salmon. They are pressure canned.

We grow chickens for eggs and meat, but mostly for eggs. I can hunt for deer and turkey here but haven't yet. We buy a local pasture-raised pig, cut and wrapped about every nine months.

We buy some local produce, mostly fruit from a certified organic farm. We have our own 60' x 60' garden; we have our insulated cold frames that we use for fresh vegetables in the winter.

Each year we do more and more canning. We have friends with apple and pie cherry trees. Some day we may have our own but some things are difficult to grow at this altitude.

Insulated Cold Frames

How much of your old life did you leave behind? TV, movies, shopping at the mall, internet, vacations, vehicles; anything you want to add here would be great.

Vacations for sure. You can't just 'up and leave' a place with animals without someone to watch them. Our Anatolian shepherd guard dog has at least allowed us to leave for short periods of time.

Otherwise the only thing that is really different is the convenience of living so close to everything including: doctors, hospitals, food, entertainment—even just driving to see family and friends.

Who had the easiest time adjusting and why?

Laurie. She is extremely self-sufficient; if she never saw another person on this planet that would be okay with her. She is very friendly and likes people but she also really likes the peace and solitude of living here.

When did you know, with as much certainty as possible, that you had made the right decision?

It's been harder than I thought it would be, because of our financial situation, starting a new business and all, but neither one of us has ever regretted it.

That being said, I think after our second year we felt better about all of our choices and research. We had enough experience to know that everything was working out the way it was originally intended.

Did your circle of friends change? Did you lose friends over this change in your lives, gain new ones?

We aren't real social people but we do have a few friends. Both of us have kept in touch mostly via the Internet and Facebook. Some friends visit every year. A few have slid away. We travel back to our hometown to visit family a few times a year.

We have met new people here; just a few like-minded folks doing something similar to what we are doing. We keep meeting more and more people who are coming here to do the same thing we are—from the same place that we came from!

They hear about us through our blog site and contact us and ask if they can come up and see our place to get ideas. It's been a lot of fun.

What are the greatest rewards you have experienced in your life because of your decision to change your lifestyle?

When I was a lot younger I wanted to homestead via the Homestead Act (I missed it by one year!) I've always wanted to do something similar to this.

We both like being more self-sufficient than we were before. We both enjoy healthier living and better food. Having far less negative impact on the environment is rewarding as well.

What is the biggest challenge you have faced?

Definitely starting a new business this late in our careers, and in a down economy.

Did you experience any issues with building codes/municipal laws that hindered your set-up in regards to building/land use/septic or other permits?

The local jurisdictions here are much easier to work with than most of the larger municipalities I have encountered in the construction trades over the years. There is no comparison.

> **Always check with your local building authority prior to purchasing your property to ensure you will be able to use the property as you wish!**

If there were three pieces of advice that you would give someone considering making this lifestyle change, what would they be?

1. Do your homework. There is as much information as you need today to make this kind of change. Learn from others who have gone before you.

2. Be prepared to make some changes to the way you live. It is going to be different. Study those differences and commit to them before you make such a large change in your life.

3. A sustainable lifestyle is harder than a convenient one. Make sure you have the right perspective and commitment and if you have a partner you both have to have the same level of commitment.

Do you feel that you have gained much more in your life than you gave up? Please explain.

We believe our life is more meaningful in this lifestyle. There is more appreciation for the things we need to live and for all of the things around us. We are more aware of where things come from that give us sustenance and comfort. Our partnership is stronger because of the mutual sacrifice and teamwork required in this lifestyle.

Have you started any new hobbies since you made the move, and if so, how did you discover your newfound interest(s)?

ED: No new hobbies for me but there has been a satisfying change of going back to doing almost everything ourselves instead of hiring them to be done for us. I do my own maintenance on equipment instead of going to a mechanic's garage.

Growing our own food and having chickens is new. All repairs on the buildings or anything like fences are done by us. We cut all our own wood. I got away from fishing for a long time and now I've taken it up again.

LAURIE: Since our winters are long and cold here you have to plan to be indoors a lot. And with travel not being a good idea unless it really is necessary, we stay home except for our once-a-week trip to town for groceries and mail pick-up.

I am what people would call a "fiber artist". I love to sew and make tote/shopping bags to sell. I also love to work with wool and make locker hook rugs. I have a tapestry loom that I will get up and working (hopefully this winter) for making wool rugs on. I do lots of quilting, felting, sewing and anything else that takes my fancy. There are just so many wonderful avenues to explore out there with fabric and fibers.

To be honest these are not new hobbies, just hobbies and interests that I have had for years, with not enough time to explore them all. Now I have long winter days to work with these things and keep myself busy.

How did you make a living prior to your move?

Whenever the economy struggles—construction takes the biggest hit. I have been through two other tough economic times in the past thirty years. It seems every ten years or so we have a slowdown.

This time it was different. We didn't just slow down. My business ceased to exist. There was no call for commercial masonry buildings anymore. Like many others, we took a big hit.

Our company became worthless almost overnight. We couldn't sell it so we just shut it down and sold the equipment and took the loss.

Please share with our readers your experience in starting a home-based business.

We did a lot of research and even spent money on professionals for a second opinion of opening an ecommerce site online and working from home. There were many success stories out there from others who were doing it.

We chose a theme that was going to be compatible with our new lifestyle and created an ecommerce site:

> ### Good Ideas for Life
> ### GoodIdeasforlife.com or
> ### http://GoodIdeasforLife.com/

To promote trust with the public we chose products we mostly use ourselves. That way we could vouch for them personally and answer any questions that potential customers might have.

We sell products that allow you to grow your own fresh food at home even if you live in a condo or apartment.

We carry small chicken coops for the backyard; emergency products for when the power goes out temporarily; water purifiers for clean drinking water; reusable canning lids and even automatic sprouters.

Is there something about your business that sets you apart from others in the same niche?

Several things come to mind:

- All of our products promote healthier living.
- We either thoroughly research our products or already use them ourselves.
- Our customer service is second to none and we are very competitive, two reasons we are growing at a really nice pace even in these difficult times.

I (Ed) also started blogging for Mother Earth News to share our new homestead lifestyle successes and/or failures with anyone else who might be interested.

Through this experience we created another website where you can see pictures and articles of everything we have experienced called:

> **Off Grid Works**
> **OffGridWorks.com or**
> **http://OffGridWorks.com/**

You can also find Laurie and Ed on Facebook at:

> **http://www.facebook.com/goodideasforlife**

Is there anything else about your home that you would like to share with our readers?

Our home has so many features I almost can't recall them all:
- Solar power with backup propane generator;
- Built out of concrete and metal, non-combustible materials so we can survive a forest fire (we already have);
- Earthquake resistant – for just a few dollars more;
- Extra switches to turn off our outlets to reduce phantom power from all appliances;
- Solar tubes for increased lighting without turning on the lights;

- Water cisterns at the barn and house to collect roof run-off so we don't have to pump well water for our horses or garden;
- Masonry heater, which is highly efficient and burns less wood than a woodstove;
- Custom built in masonry kitchen stove with a 42" cast iron top;
- Tank-less hot water heater;
- Our own cell phone system (there is no signal here);
- Home-made insulated curtains;
- Our roof overhang is calculated to let the sun in to help heat our home during the winter months and keep the sun out during the hot summer to help cool the house;
- Our garage is underground 6' on one side and the attached heated house on the other side. The result is that it never freezes and makes a perfect food storage area.

Ed graciously agreed to share a recent blog that he wrote which goes into more detail about their property and its features.

House Design Feature List

Our off-grid home has many design features you don't normally find in most houses. Many people come here to see what some of these features look like or how they operate. Since I seem to struggle with my memory more and more I thought it would be nice to list them out along with a little explanation of them.

(You can visit Ed's blog for more detail on most of these features.)

• Roof overhangs – our eave length is calculated to keep the sun out of the windows in the summer, which helps with natural cooling, and lets the sun in during the colder winter months, which helps with passive heating. Anyone can do the calculation. It is most important for the south side of the house.

• ICF'S – the exterior walls are made out of Styrofoam concrete forms filled with concrete. The concrete is 8" thick. I personally recommend that if you go this route you need to use the ICF's that have more insulation on the outside form than on the inside, especially in colder climates.

• Earthquake-proof – because we chose to have a concrete slab and concrete walls it was relatively inexpensive to add enough rebar to make it possible to withstand a pretty good size earthquake. We've already had a 5+ on the Richter scale.

• Fire-proof – our exterior walls are layered with Hardiplank siding, then 2" of 3 hour, fire-treated ICF, then 8" concrete and then another 2" of 3 hour treated ICF. Our roof is metal. Our soffits are also metal with tiny slots for venting. We also put metal ceilings on the exposed wood framing in the carport and front porch roofs. This makes our house virtually immune to forest fires. We were tested the very first year we moved in. We had zero repercussions.

• Solar tubes – these allow natural light where you wouldn't normally have any. They greatly reduce the need for electrical lighting.

• Water cisterns—we have three of them. They capture water off the roof of the house and barn and store it. We use the stored water for our garden (low pressure gravity flow) and to water the horses. We have been able to do both of those tasks for 11 months of the year without using our solar power to run the well pump.

• We have a three-sided attached wood shed and a carport with two open sides and a garage with a large door. We put regular wall footings in the ground along the open sides of those two structures and at the garage door opening. In the future, if we want to, we can install a framed, insulated wall in those openings and double the size of our house.

• Masonry heater—our custom masonry heater only burns about five cords of wood each year to heat our home and we live at an elevation of 4200'. The winter temperatures get down below zero. It is extremely efficient at over 95%.

• Wood burning kitchen stove—we also have a custom built masonry kitchen stove with a 42" cooktop that burns wood. We also use it to heat the house in the spring and fall when it is only mildly cold. When the stove isn't already going we just use the regular propane stove to cook with and use the 42" cast iron top as counter space.

• Solar power—we produce all of our own electricity with a photovoltaic solar power system with batteries and inverter. We also have a backup generator that runs about 100 hours per year when it clouds up for a period of time.

• Insulated cold frames—on the south side of the house we put in raised bed insulated cold frames. We have grown fresh cold weather type vegetables as cold as 18F with nothing to heat them but the sun. They are attached to the side of the house which never freezes.

• Plug in switches—we have more wall switches than most

homes. The extra switches turn our phantom power off when an appliance isn't being used. Phantom power consists of things like the stereo and microwave clocks or anything else that shows lit up on a screen even though the appliance is turned off.

• HRV—we have a whole house fan for fresh air that is configured to warm up the incoming cold air with the outgoing heated air. The result is semi-heated fresh air which becomes pretty important in the winter months when we have to keep our house warm.

• Tank-less hot water heater—our hot water heater has a little generator in the supply line that lights the propane pilot light when the water is turned on.

• Outdoor sink—we have a commercial food prep sink outside we can use during the months that aren't freezing. It is great for cleaning the garden veggies, and cleaning fish and the chickens at butcher time. This sink helps keep all the mess outside. In the winter month we just drain the lines.

• Outside generator/ pump switch—we added another switch and plug-in for pumping water from the carport. If I don't want to use my solar power to run the 220V deep well pump I can hook my little portable generator to an outside plug-in and flip the bypass switch and pump water from the carport. This comes in handy during the cloudy months. This won't be such a big deal when we get our new pump which only uses 1/3 of the amperage to run as our existing pump but I will still have the option.

• Cell phone system—there is no cell coverage here but we have managed to acquire a signal via a system of cell phone amplifiers and antennas.

• Insulated curtains—Laurie made all new curtains for the

house that are insulated to an R value of 5. That doesn't seem like much until you close them during the cold months. You can feel the difference immediately. I believe they save us about two cords of wood each year.

• Sun Frost refrigerator—these are expensive but well worth the money if you are off-grid. They don't run near as often as a traditional fridge. The reason is that they are well insulated and the compressor is located at the top instead of the bottom like all other conventional fridges. Compressors put out heat. When they are located at the bottom of the appliance they warm it up which causes it to run in order to cool it back down. This is a ridiculously simple concept.

• Appliances—look at the electrical use in terms of watts or amperage to compare appliances when choosing which ones to buy. Even then it is tricky. Our dishwasher, vacuum, and chest freezer are the biggest electrical hogs.

• Garage temperature—we even have an unintended design feature in the garage. One side is underground 6' and the other side is a heated wall from the house. The result is that it never freezes and is the perfect temperature for food storage in the winter. It's just like a root cellar!

Be sure to read Ed's blog for more information and tips for living off-grid at:

http://www.motherearthnews.com/blogs/
blog.aspx?blogid=1510&tag=Ed%20Essex

One final question—do you have any closing thoughts you would like to leave with our readers?

You can make a difference in your life, the environment, and those around you no matter where you live.

We started practicing conservation in our condo before we moved. We cut our power and water usage about 20%. We paid more attention to recycling. We bought used items instead of new whenever we could.

> **You don't have to make the drastic change that we did to make a difference.**

✳ ✳ ✳

A Way of Life Less Common

McElmurray's Mountain Retreat

Carol & Bruce McElmurray
with Echo, Sarah, Gypsy and Bozwell

Carol and Bruce live on 11 majestic acres in the Colorado mountains. With two natural springs to attract wildlife and a greenbelt behind to ensure privacy, their piece of paradise also boasts an A-frame cabin that keeps the McElmurray's and their four dogs cozy and happy all year long.

McElmurray's Mountain Retreat

*B*ruce bought the property (that he and Carol now call home) back in 1978, sight unseen. The folks he contacted via telephone asked him whether he wanted to *be* in the mountains or if he wanted to *see* the mountains. He said, "In the mountains."

Bruce had never seen the property, so in 1984 they made a trip from Florida to Colorado and fell in love—instantly. They planned to *someday* build on the property and eventually retire in Colorado. That *someday* eventually came, and in 1990, the shell was built by a local contractor. They spent their vacations putting in the plumbing, electricity, walls, insulation, etc.

Their entire dream became reality in 1997 when Bruce took an early retirement and they retired to the mountains full-time.

Making the choice to homestead, live off-grid and/or live in the bush is a life changing decision. What initially led you to make this choice?

Our decision was based on our love for peace and quiet and remote living, and enjoying each other's company.

Prior to making this decision, were you already familiar with this lifestyle? Were you outdoor-lovers? Farmers or gardeners? Hunters? Working at home? Campers?

We love camping and hiking. Bruce *was* a hunter but not anymore, now that he has made friends with much of the wildlife that is in our area. Bruce always wanted to have a garden and now he does!

What were your biggest concerns, fears or other factors that you had to consider?

We really had no concerns but were very anxious to start on the next phase of our lives. Others had concerns for us, mainly being far away from medical services and neighbors. Trips to town, 45 miles one way, had to be carefully planned, and services were at a distance, so additional planning had to be done.

How long was it, from the time you made the decision to the time you actually made the move, and why?

We started saving money (not going out to eat, movies, etc.)

from the time we visited the property in 1984 until we had the contractor start the cabin in 1990. The only thing that kept us from making the move sooner was that we wanted to have enough money set aside to keep us going on a small pension and retire with medical benefits.

How did your family react? Please include the reactions of immediate family as well as extended family if possible.

I believe that most of our family thought we were crazy, moving so far away from them. They are spread out on the east coast.

How did you get the process started? For instance, did you need to save money, change jobs, search for property in another area of the country or buy property in another country?

After we saw the property and decided to retire in Colorado, we saved money so that we would not have any large outstanding debts when we retired.

How did you know that you had found the perfect property?

We knew that Bruce had found the perfect property, sight unseen, when we made our first visit to Colorado. It was a beautiful piece of mountain property. The property Bruce chose had a green belt behind it to insure no one would ever build behind us. It has two, year round springs on the property which attract wild life and birds.

It was more than we had hoped for.

Were you nervous about your decision, and if so, why?

We made the decision and have never had a second thought.

What were your intentions? To go off grid? Become self-sufficient? Escape the rat race?

We mainly wanted to escape the rat race and live a simpler, less stressful life.

Can you describe your land and the cabin you built?

We bought 5.5 acres of raw land on a mountainside with lots of trees. We also purchased a 5.5 acre adjacent lot.

Our home is a small, 850 square foot A-frame cabin. The cabin has an open floor plan with a large living area, a sleeping loft, one bathroom, a small kitchen, pantry, breakfast room, mudroom and a partial basement, detached garage, and wood shed. We live at an elevation of 9750 feet.

What influenced your design choices in the construction of your cabin?

We chose a small dwelling since we are only two people and figured we didn't need a large home. We figured that a small home would be easier to maintain, heat, and less home to be cleaning constantly.

What was the biggest surprise once you made the move?

It was a surprise to realize that we had finally achieved our goal. We had dreamed and prayed for this for years, but to then wake up and look around—we were stunned that it all came together as well as it did.

What is the biggest thing you wish you had done differently right from the beginning?

I wish we had realized that someday we would get old and things like stairs would eventually become an issue.

Has there ever been a time since you made the move that you wished you hadn't? What happened to make you feel this way and how did you deal with these emotions or situations?

No. We have no regrets over our decision. Perhaps our greatest future regret is that one day we will have to sell our home due to aging and the inability to cope with the environment.

How much did your life change on a daily routine basis? Did you go from working in an office in a downtown setting to getting up every morning and gardening/chopping wood/ etc...?

Prior to the move Bruce worked in an office setting a few miles from our home. I stayed at home after working in different areas.

Our life changed drastically. We get up and go to bed when

we want to and decide what we are going to do each day, instead of *someone else* telling us what we will do.

Our life went from city living to self-sufficiency and yes, we do cut our own firewood, which works out to about 11 cords per winter. We heat with a wood stove.

What appliances and other household items did you choose not to have and why? Which ones did you choose to keep and why?

The only appliances that most homes have that we do not, are a clothes dryer and an automatic dishwasher. When we lived in the city, I did not use the dishwasher (except for storage) and I prefer to hang our clean laundry outside or, in the winter time, in our sleeping loft. We do have all the other basic appliances anyone could want.

Are there any items of furniture/appliances/tools/vehicles that you use that you absolutely would not give up?

We have a Jeep and a truck—we would give up neither. We would not give up the Kubota tractor and accessories, or our computers, or the microwave. Actually I don't think we would give up anything we have.

We evaluated our needs before we ever made the move and we chose those items that we knew we would use often, like our chainsaws and other survival tools. If anything was questionable regarding usefulness, we did not include it in our plan.

Bruce is pretty skilled in preventative maintenance on our equipment and takes good care of it; therefore our equipment has lasted us for a long time.

What are the most useful items that you use? This could be something like a snowmobile/ATV or even something as simple as a kitchen utensil that makes your life easier/more enjoyable. More than one item is welcome here.

Probably the most useful item we have is the Kubota tractor. It has a blade as well as a snow thrower and a wood chipper.

We were given a small trailer that helps us haul wood and limbs for mulching. We could not live here without the tractor and attachments. Since we heat with wood, our chain saws and newly purchased log splitter are essential and would be hard to survive without. They are very useful.

How do you heat your home, power your home, wash clothes, cook, and obtain water?

We heat mainly with a woodstove; we have electricity, a clothes washer, a small propane stove and a deep well for water.

What do you miss from your old life (if anything)?

I'm not sure we miss anything except being closer to family and friends. With our computers and the ability to Skype, staying in touch is easier. Beyond that I don't believe we miss much from our old life.

What is the some of the challenges you've faced after making the move?

Learning to bake at an elevation of 9750 feet!

Having to slow down was also an adjustment. The air is thinner at this altitude and you need to really approach tasks slower or you will get out of breath quickly.

How did you provide food for your family? Did you continue to shop at grocery stores/frequent farmer's markets/barter/grow your own?

Bruce grows some food in the garden boxes—spinach, lettuce, rhubarb, Swiss chard—but our growing season is really short.

We shop at a grocery store a couple of times a month and visit Sam's Club in Pueblo (a two hour drive, one-way) twice a year.

How much of your old life did you leave behind? TV, movies, shopping at the mall, internet, vacations, or even vehicles?

We never were big movie-goers or mall shoppers and really didn't leave anything behind—except a lot of stress and aggravation.

In your immediate family, who had the most difficult time adjusting and why?

If you are talking about Bruce and I being the immediate family—I would have to guess me. It is difficult sometimes not to have any female friends living right down the road to chat with or go to lunch with. However, I am thankful for the internet and Skype, which have kept me in the loop with girlfriends and family. We are both very comfortable with our surroundings and who we are and we adjusted almost immediately.

There was so much work to be done when we moved here full-time (like getting our firewood in and clearing debris from around the cabin) that we really didn't have time to worry about adjustment. We have stayed busy ever since.

Who had the easiest time adjusting and why?

Living this lifestyle is what Bruce had looked forward to for a very long time, so adjusting was pretty easy for him. We are both content with our lifestyle, and being together is a large part of our happiness.

When did you know, with as much certainty as possible, that you had made the right decision?

Immediately!

Was there was ever a time when you felt like you had made the wrong decision; when was it and why did you feel that way?

Not really. There are a variety of people who live in our community. Many try to bring all the amenities into the wilderness that they had in the big city and have different attitudes about life and community. We pretty much stay by ourselves, as small talk and progressive ideas are not part of the lifestyle we choose.

Did your circle of friends change? Did you lose friends over this change in your lives, gain new ones?

Actually, we still have our old friends and remain in touch with them regularly. We both do volunteer work and because of the vast number of people we have encountered doing that work, we have a large circle of friends outside of our immediate community. Bruce volunteers for a German shepherd dog rescue and I volunteer for Global Media Outreach. I have a broad number of varied communities I work with on a daily basis and have made numerous friends through that volunteerism.

What are the greatest rewards you have experienced in your life because of your decision to change your lifestyle.?

Probably the knowledge that we are very self-sufficient people and that we can be happy under difficult circumstances. In the city there is far less need to be self-reliant. I have learned to do many things that I never thought I would be doing or could do.

What are the biggest challenges you have faced?

Perhaps the silence and isolation; in the winter when the snow falls it is so quiet that you are initially stunned by the absolute silence. Going outside with our dogs at night and looking up and seeing the stars is awesome. In the city we were never aware that there were so many stars. It is a big challenge to realize how tiny we actually are in the universe. It is an awesome experience and helps to put ourselves into perspective.

Did you experience any issues with building codes/municipal laws that hindered your set-up in regards to building/land use/septic or other permits?

Our county is so small that it was easy to work with those who handle codes. In fact they were a great help in keeping us from making mistakes that we would have later regretted.

If there were three pieces of advice that you would give some-one considering making this lifestyle change, what would they be?

We were young-ish when we built our cabin and didn't think of a few things that would affect us as we got older. One—we have realized that a one-story cabin would have been a much better choice—no stairs. Two—our sleeping habits have changed; our loft is our bedroom with no doors to shut out the light when one of us is up at night. Three—we should have considered having a 2nd sleeping area.

Back of
Bruce and Carol's
A-Frame Cabin

Do you feel that you have gained much more in your life than you gave up? Please explain.

We have gained some much needed relief from a busy and stressful lifestyle, enjoying fresh air, silence and clean water. Our gains far exceed our losses.

Most people dream of this type of lifestyle and here we are, living it daily. It has completed our lives and when either of us comes to the end of our life, I don't believe we will have any regrets. It is a lifestyle for completion of your life, not an interruption of your life.

> *Living like we do fulfills our lives in ways*
> *you could not expect or wish for.*

Have you started any new hobbies since you made the move, and if so, how did you discover your newfound interest(s)?

Bruce has been able to do a lot more of his wood working and I have found that being an online missionary is a real blessing. Also Bruce has been able to have his garden.

How did you make a living prior to your move and what do you do now?

Bruce was a supervisor at an insurance company and for a couple of years prior to our move, I stayed at home; prior to that I worked in various capacities. We do not have a business now.

Are there any final thoughts you would like to share with our readers?

Use common sense and do not take just one person's opinion. Get as much input as you can before making decisions. For example, one person told us we should get an electric stove. Oftentimes the electricity goes out, here in the mountains—sometimes for a few days. We are very thankful we did not listen to his advice. Our small propane stove and oven do not need electricity at all!

People have diverse opinions but you need to weigh what you are told with reality. We took known challenges one at a time and discussed them thoroughly and thought them through. We made the best decisions for our lifestyle.

If you would like to read more about Carol and Bruce's experiences, you can follow up through the web links below.

Carol and Bruce's website can be found at:

http://www.brucecarolcabin.blogspot.com

Bruce's articles can be seen
(under the Happy Homesteader icon) at:

http://www.motherearthnews.com

We are always happy to share our experiences with others!

artifex41@gmail.com (Bruce)
bamcam83@gmail.com (Carol)

✳✳✳

Beyond Ordinary

Deborah & Ross Hinter

From 2008 to 2012, Ross and Deborah Hinter enjoyed life in a modest log cabin at the edge of the boreal forest, happily living with no electricity, running water or indoor toilet.

Using alternative energy, they were comfortable, yet challenged in their everyday life. They believe that their kinship with the simple life in the bush cultivated a deeper understanding of the early ways.

Beyond Ordinary

*R*oss Hinter is a wildlife conservationist, craftsman and educator. He grew up in British Columbia and raised his family of five children while working as a cowboy on the ranches of the Cariboo and the Nicola Valley.

As a young man from the Lower Mainland in Cloverdale, BC, he had a yearning to go into the bush to follow the tracks of animals and quickly became attuned to their world.

Ross believes that our relationship with nature is intertwined, and is not just something we observe. His desire is to better understand, respect and take care of each other and our environment.

Ross's journey has led him down numerous paths that included some exciting projects in TV and the media.

These successes however, pale in comparison to one of his greatest accomplishments. Ross has helped over 9000 students young and old, begin to walk the path of wisdom and gain respect for the natural world; this he considers a great privilege.

He could easily have lived in the mountains with Jeremiah Johnson.

Deborah Hinter is a wife, mother and administrative professional. She grew up in southern Ontario, and spent summers on the family's homestead in the rural backwoods of New Brunswick.

She has 4 children and has called many parts of Canada home. Law firms, government offices, and oil sand projects were a source of livelihood, while she yearned for simpler times remembered on the dirt roads of River de Chute, NB. She lived in the world of offices, longing for a hundred years ago.

Finding herself a widow at the age of 52, she looked at this time in her life, as "the gift of change" Returning to a wood cook stove, lamp light, outhouse and no indoor plumbing, held great appeal.

Meeting Ross and moving to the log cabin was the reality of living it. Though filled with challenges, the off-grid life without the constant flash of LED lights and the hum of appliances was welcome.

The experience of "listening" to the silence was a gift.

Making the choice to homestead, live off-grid and/or live in the bush is a life changing decision. What initially led you to make this choice?

Ross: Something I had always planned to do.
Deborah: Marrying Ross and sharing the same desires for simplicity.

Prior to making this decision, were you already familiar with this lifestyle? Were you outdoor-lovers? Farmers or gardeners? Hunters? Working at home? Campers?

Ross: Yes, as long as I can remember I would find some bush to go to play in. I always found jobs that would take me in the bush.
Deborah: Yes, from early childhood summers spent in backwoods in New Brunswick on the family homestead. Camping was the number one activity of joy for my entire family.

What were your biggest concerns, fears or other factors that you had to consider?

Ross: Finding a woman that would live like I wanted too!!
Deborah: The darkest nights imaginable, (I'm scared of the dark), being alone while Ross was away working, and not to mention my terrifying dreams of being attacked by a black bear. I was also afraid of people that might be out on a joy ride down a back road—finding me alone. I took my firearm training and obtained my license to operate firearms, which gave me greater confidence

that I would be able to scare off a bear from getting into our cabin.

How long was it, from the time you made the decision to the time you actually made the move?

Ross: It was a gradual process I guess. Living out in cow camps and staying in trap-line cabins and working out in the bush. Finally after my children grew up and I was alone I sold my farm and found this place.
Deborah: When I met Ross.

How did your family react? Please include the reactions of immediate family as well as extended family if possible.

Ross: No one was surprised.
Deborah: Mom said, "Are you sure about this???????"

How did you know that you had found the perfect property?

Ross: It just felt right. I went back a second time to look at it and I liked it even more than the first time.

Were you nervous about your decision, and if so, why?

Ross: I knew I was in for a lot of work and didn't really want to be alone, so the worry of finding a woman that would make the move and be able to handle it made me nervous.

What were your intentions? To go off-grid? Become self-sufficient? Escape the rat race?

Ross: I liked the idea of being off-grid for sure. I have never done well trying to live to close to cities. This place was on the edge of crown land with a good mix of northern boreal forest where I could travel for miles by snow machine or quad or horseback.

Did you buy a property with a home/cabin already in place? Why did you make that choice?

Ross: Yes, the cabin was already built and the property had a workshop and storage shed on it. It was built of logs (nothing fancy), and small enough to be easy to heat in the winter.

What was the biggest surprise once you made the move? This could either be something funny or something not-so-funny.

Ross: Getting rid of four porcupines that were living under the cabin and then trying to convince my dog to let me take care of them my own way!!

Deborah: Bats, and more bats—being up at 1:00am, sitting outside in my Lexus, while my brave hero fought them off inside the cabin. We had been sitting comfortably up in the loft using our laptops when they came swooping up the stairs, and we both hit the deck. I was *strongly* encouraged to go outside to sit and wait in my Lexus while Ross got the situation under control. After eviction, we then stuffed steel wool into the crevices that we could find and then—the best part of all—sitting down together at 2am at the kitchen table and sharing a celebratory glass of scotch!

The Hinter's Cabin Kitchen

Have you ever wished you hadn't made the move? What happened and how did you deal with these emotions or situations?

Ross: No. Lots of trials and things to deal with but that's what makes living out here so interesting!

Deborah: In January of 2009, Ross was lying in the hospital with a life threatening illness, and I wished fervently at that time that we didn't live so far out, with no land line, no hot running water and no close neighbours.

You come to a place over time when you begin to stop fearing the worst and begin enjoying each moment. You become conscious of the amount of gasoline you need for the generator so you can keep a cell phone charged up; you make sure you have gas in your tank to get you to the nearest hospital, and you double check the amount of water you have left in your jugs.

Please share information about your property, such as the amount of land you purchased and type of building you live in.

Ross: The amount of land was only three and a half acres but it is the last piece of private land on a dead end road next to endless boreal forest which is my back yard. The cabin we live in is just about 740sq ft., built of logs. It has a loft and this also includes the little addition (I needed a bedroom if I was to keep a woman happy).

Dead-End Road to Property

The fellow that built the place built another log building that was to be the log home, but it wasn't built as well as the cabin. I use it for a shop and storage. I have a generator to run some power tools etc., if I need them in this building. Both buildings were wired for power. I assume he hoped one day to get on the grid, but it never happened, so we just plug in our generator when we want to use power tools. I sold my little farm just before I bought this place and decided I would buy a good generator while I had the money—I am sure glad I did.

How much did your life change on a daily routine basis?

Deborah: Life changed dramatically. I went from high heels and corporate offices, to blue jeans, muck boots and bug spray. No flipping a switch to get heat.

Your wonderful husband supplies you with a good amount of firewood on the front porch and if you run out while he's gone, you have a wagon for fall, and a sleigh for winter, to go get a fresh supply.

Deborah & Ross' Woodburning Cookstove

You learn that sleeping through the night at 47 below zero is *not* a good idea and you become attuned to getting up a couple times a night to stoke the stove.

Having a bath is big deal—we went from sponge baths in a big basin—to my (delightful) find of a rubber feed trough at the local hardware store, bathing in the midst of a thunderstorm on the porch and then watching a beautiful rainbow—to the old cast iron tub placed in front on the porch, complete with mosquito coils, red wine and spa bath oil on the chair (for atmosphere)—to the ultimate treasure—an old galvanized cowboy tub at an antique mall in Edmonton.

Feed Trough Bathtub

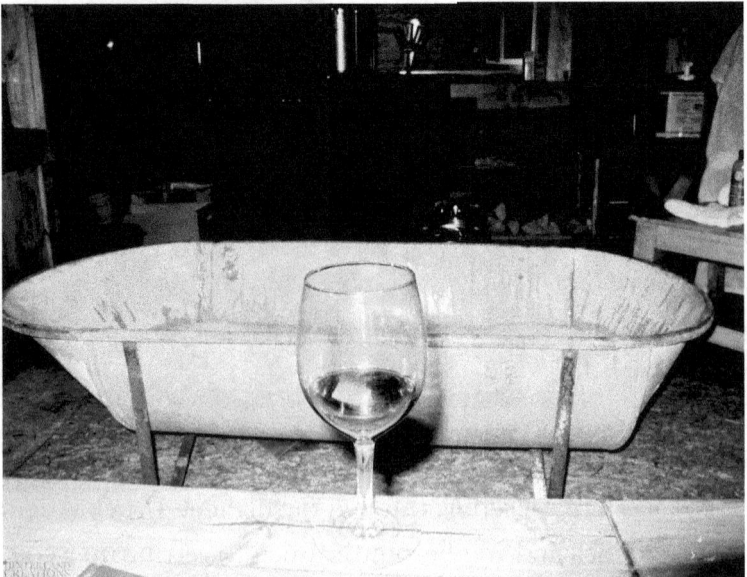

Antique Cowboy Bathtub

In the early days in summer, Ross would carry jugs down to the well, and hand-pump them all full, heat them up on the outdoor Yukon burner and pour them into whichever tub we wanted to use that evening. In winter, we would haul jugs of water from family and town.

Later we kept large pots of boiling water on the new Amish wood cook stove, and then graduated to a well pump and then a portable, hot water on-demand system that ran on propane.

What appliances and other household items did you choose not to have and why? Which ones did you choose to keep and why?

Ross: Well Deb's listed most of it. We really didn't need much.

Deborah: Cable TV, nothing much interested us, no time to sit there and watch it, so we enjoyed videos that we purchased, and many of them were of the outdoors and people living life differently!

We did without crock pots, rice cookers, and electric frying pans, and toaster ovens.

I kept my hair blower, curling iron and flat iron. A gal's gotta have what a gal needs!

We also kept the vacuum which was used when the generator was running. You had to plan ahead, and when it was on, you ran around doing as much as you could with the power before turning it off again.

Solar energy changes all that!

Are there any items of furniture/appliances/tools/vehicles that you use that you absolutely would not give up?

Deborah: My MacBook Pro and external monitor and the internet. It's how I now earned income from home and stayed connected to my family and friends.

Fresh ground coffee beans in the morning! Before we got the solar system, someone had to make the trek out to the generator and fire it up so we could grind our coffee beans.

What are the most useful items that you use? This could be something like a snowmobile/ATV or even something as simple as a kitchen utensil that makes your life easier/more enjoyable.

Ross: Chainsaw, Honda generator and snow shovel!

Deborah: A port-a-potty for night time use—no need to tempt the boogie man; a wringer washer, a Danby washer spin dryer, a log splitter, steel wool, large pots, long johns, thick wool socks to wear inside, lace up moccasins, my cameras, solar powered radio and battery packs to charge up cell phones.

How do you heat your home, power your home, wash clothes, cook, and obtain water?

Ross: We have a bored well, 53ft deep—we used a hand pump until we finally got a well pump that I could run with the generator to fill a 55 gallon tank at the cabin (that stores our water for the week). We have a Baker's Choice wood cook stove that has a big fire box that heats the cabin all night.

We also have a propane cook stove for cooking when it's too hot to use the wood cook stove. We have a Honda 6500 watt inverter for power. We now have a solar system to run the cabin so we don't have to use the generator much.

Deborah: Everything was originally washed in a Lehman's mobile breathing washer in a galvanized laundry tub on the porch; we then went to a wringer washer and a dual set of laundry tubs on wheels and finally to a Danby electric washer, spin dryer.

What do you miss from your old life?

Ross: I guess maybe conveniences. Being closer to family.

Deborah: Going to Starbucks whenever I wanted and my front load LG washer and dryer. Starbucks had this ability to make me feel connected to the rest of humanity and its activities. Laundry was always a challenge for me. I really missed my friends and family, who were all so far away.

What is the biggest challenge you faced after making the move?

Deborah: Bats!

How did you provide food for your family? Did you continue to shop at grocery stores/frequent farmer's markets/barter/grow your own? Please specify for both produce and meat/fish.

Deborah: Grocery stores and the local Hutterite Colony.

If there was ever a time when you felt like you had made the wrong decision, when was it and why did you feel that way?

Deborah: Very early on, I recall lying on the couch in the cabin crying, wondering how I would fit in to this new life. I felt in many ways ill-equipped to live off the grid and didn't know if I could do it well.

Did your circle of friends change? Did you lose friends over this change in your lives, gain new ones? Please elaborate.

Deborah: We did grow close to the local Hutterite colony and the women there were so very kind to me and very interested in this gal who lived in a cabin in the bush with the bears! My old friends did make the yearly trek to visit my life in the bush, which was such a gift to me

What are the greatest rewards you have experienced in your life because of your decision to change your lifestyle?

Ross: Solitude and privacy. Making things work ourselves. The connection to nature and the bush.

Deborah: Learning how to stop doing and start being. Overcoming my fear of wildlife and learning how to safely handle firearms. Gaining an understanding of how much water one really needs, and the delight of knowing that you just produced your own power from solar panels and batteries. Simple as that—sure brings a smile.

What is the biggest thing you wish you had done differently right from the beginning?

Ross: Made sure the guy I bought the place from cleaned out his stuff from the buildings etc..

Deborah: Nothing, every part of the journey was there to teach us.

If there were three pieces of advice that you would give some-one considering making this lifestyle change, what would they be?

Deborah: Do your homework, never give up on your dreams and be realistic

Do you feel that you have gained much more in your life than you gave up?

Deborah: You learn to slow down and take your time. NOTHING happens quickly off the grid. When you live at the dead end of a county dirt road, you realize that you have entered a shift from the highways and streets of towns and cities.

How did you make a living prior to your move and what do you do now?

Ross: Wildlife control. Teaching bush living skills etc..

Deborah: My income was earned from the corporate world and office work. Now I develop a blog and YouTube channel and earn income from advertisers.

I like to spend about ten hours a day with it, from shooting video, photos, editing and creative writing; then the technical tasks of uploading and formatting, as well as developing the advertising appeal of my channel.

Ten hours a day however is unrealistic when one lives off the grid and you take into consideration all the time required to attend to your own daily needs.

You can find Deborah and Ross on YouTube at:

North Trapping and Bush Life

http://www.youtube.com/user/campfirepoetry

Their blog, Beyond Ordinary, Life On and Off the Grid at:

http://northtrappingandbushlife.blogspot.ca/

Are there any final thoughts you would like to share with our readers?

Ross: I guess for us we decided "to live out" as I call it, or off-grid as it is called by most because we want to be in touch with our own living as much as we could—to know and understand what is needed for daily living.

For many people their food, clothing, heat and water are provided by a system they just pay for, but don't really understand these are things we rely on and have no control of. Just to learn to make a pair of moccasins or some type of footwear from something that we gathered ourselves in order to wrap our feet helps us to connect to something bigger than we realize.

To make a pullover shirt from two deerskins may seem quite primitive but helps to gain an understanding of how little we know about **our** own needs and basic requirements.

Another example is that when you carry your daily water requirements in a bucket—you use only what you need.

When you kill an animal and clean it to eat, you gain much more reverence and respect for the death of the animal. You don't think about it when you buy your meat from a white foam tray wrapped in plastic wrap at a supermarket!

Bucksin Shirt

I have had the opportunity to be in touch with the predator-prey world of nature and experience the completeness of it at least to some degree.

To have the opportunity to experience life in this way in such a hurry-up world of today is a real privilege, as I see it. It is a grand experience for Deb and me.

I would encourage anyone who has felt the pull
and wants to experience it for their own—to go for it.

- *Ross Hinter*

***

The Walden Effect

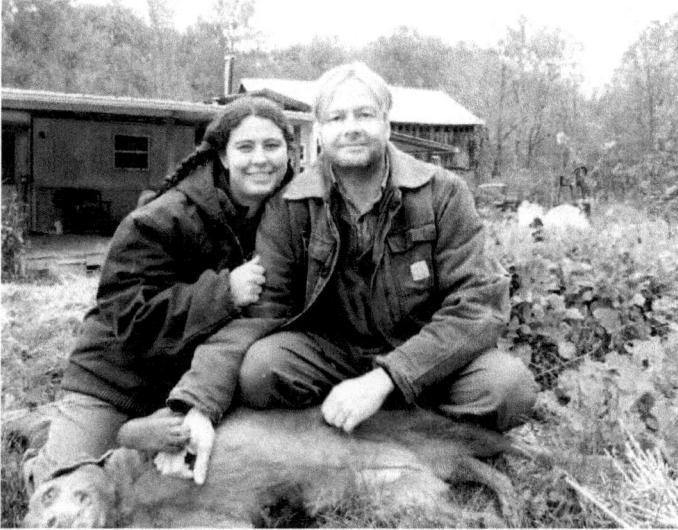

Anna Hess & Mark Hamilton

Anna and Mark are back-to-the-landers, living simply on their 58 acres of swamp and hillside in southwest Virginia.

When they arrived on the farm in September 2006, a hundred year old barn stood amid a mass of blackberries and honeysuckle so thick they could hardly push their way through. Since then, they've cleared a couple of acres (leaving the rest of the forest to grow naturally toward its climax state), installed a free trailer to live in, and are learning to farm.

The Walden Effect

*A*nna Hess was trained as a biologist and now turns her scientific leanings toward experimenting with no-till gardening, mushroom propagation, and chicken pasturing.

She dreamed about moving back into the countryside ever since her parents dragged her kicking and screaming from their family farm at the ripe old age of eight. She admits that her childhood memories of farming don't really match reality—real farm life involves a lot more hard work than the eight year old was involved in! But the reality is also much more fulfilling and she loves harvesting her own vegetables, pigging out on sun-warmed strawberries, and soaking in a washtub of water in the yard.

She has published one paperback, *The Weekend Homesteader,* and a variety of ebooks on Amazon.

Mark Hamilton grew up in the suburbs in Ohio and never considered living the farm life until recently, but his family's roots lie in hard-scrabble farming in eastern Kentucky—homesteading seems to run in his blood.

While Anna putters with her seed packets and makes planting charts, Mark does the hard work of mowing, fencing, building chicken coops, and keeping the farm running smoothly.

He loves the freedom of making up his own hours and the self-sufficiency of living off the land.

Recently, he has enjoyed inventing labor-saving farm devices, including his Avian Aqua Miser—a POOP-free chicken waterer—the sales of which provide the farm's main source of income.

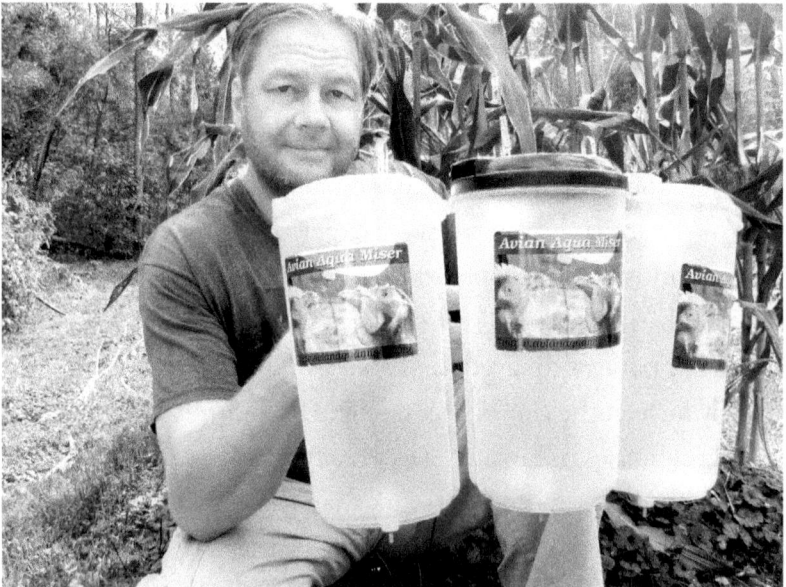

Mark and His Invention
Avian Aqua Miser
(a poop-free chicken waterer)

Making the choice to homestead, live off-grid and/or live in the bush is a life changing decision. What initially led you to make this choice?

Anna: My parents were back-to-the-landers during the 1970s, but they soon threw in the towel and moved our family back to town. I was in third grade at the time (and had permissive parents), so I'd only enjoyed the delightful parts of farm life without any of the hard work. I vowed to find my own farm then and there, and nineteen years later, I made that dream a reality.

Mark: I had been drifting from place to place looking for something different and more independent when I first met Anna. Sparks started flying from day one, and I made the decision to start putting down some roots in this beautiful region.

Prior to making this decision, were you already familiar with this lifestyle? Were you outdoor-lovers? Farmers or gardeners? Hunters? Working at home? Campers?

Anna: In addition to my early experiences with farm life, I was very much interested in the natural world. I spent a lot of time hiking during my childhood, majored in biology (and studio art) in college and then spent a year abroad, camping my way across three continents. I hadn't ever hunted though (and actually flirted with becoming a vegetarian), and I'd always had a job.

Mark: I had zero garden experience, but an intense appreciation for natural beauty. The working at home part has been a life-long dream that is littered with several failures before we settled on the Avian Aqua Miser.

What were your biggest concerns, fears or other factors that you had to consider?

Anna: I wasn't afraid of making the leap to the farm, but was terrified to quit my job. My fears weren't entirely rational, especially since I'd spent most of my life living below the poverty line and knew how to make ends meet on very little.

But it took some concerted effort on Mark's part to talk me into quitting so we'd have time to develop an independent source of income.

Mark: My biggest concern was balance. Anna had managed to buy the land at that point and I didn't have more than a hundred dollars in the bank. I would have felt more comfortable kicking in a chunk, but eventually Anna convinced me that my labor and imagination investments were more valuable than a big or medium-sized check.

How long was it, from the time you made the decision to the time you actually made the move, and why?

Anna: Although I technically spent 19 years post-decision before moving to the farm, I think the more relevant bit of data was that it took about three years after buying the farm to make the move. I hadn't met Mark yet, and was trying to tear down an already falling down house by myself. I had no experience, had to haul hand tools through half a mile of mud to get to the house site (no electricity, of course), and started out working in the bitter winter cold. I soon came down with carpal tunnel syndrome and realized I was physically unable to do the work by myself.

Luckily, Mark showed up soon thereafter and lent his strong back and creative thinking to the endeavor, so we found a free trailer and eventually moved in.

Mark: I want to say it was a bit over a year after I made the decision to be a homesteader before we got electricity hooked up and were able to move in.

How did your family react? Please include the reactions of immediate family as well as extended family if possible.

Anna: Even though I did borrow some money from a close friend to buy the farm, I wanted to stay as far out of debt as possible. So I bought what was (and is) very much an ugly duckling property.

The 'driveway' is half a mile of mud through a floodplain, crossing a creek that sometimes floods more than six feet deep and that can cut off access for days at a time.

We ended up moving into a trailer that we got for free as well, and my father, especially, hated the decision. All of the folks my parent's age thought it was crazy to move to such an inaccessible piece of land—what would I do when I was seventy, they asked? I figured that forty-some years of hard work would get the farm in shape, and six years later we're well on our way.

Mark: My mom was thrilled I had decided to settle in the same time zone while my dad was sort of indifferent—like he tends to be on most subjects.

Some of my friends scratched their heads at such a shift in direction and most still think I'm a bit crazy.

If you had children at home when you made this decision, did you include them in the process and if so, what was their reaction?

Anna: Mark and I opted not to have children for a variety of reasons. Foremost among them is our wish to live simply and spend time on creative pursuits—kids are expensive and time-consuming. We figured that since neither of us felt the biological imperative to reproduce, we'd expend our energy elsewhere.

Mark: I was very relieved when Anna announced that "kids are sticky", but I was a bit dubious.

I spent the next few years making sure there was no chance of her biological clock kicking in, and after she turned 30 it felt more real and I decided to get a vasectomy.

How did you get the process started? For instance, did you need to save money, change jobs, search for property in another area of the country or buy property in another country?

Anna: I grew up in Appalachia where land is very cheap (although jobs are often unavailable), and I knew I wanted to buy land close to home. Our ugly duckling property was only $600 per acre in 2003.

That said, I saved every penny for the three years between college and buying the land, and was lucky to get a no-interest loan from a friend for the remainder.

We just finished paying off our debt this year.

How did you know that you had found the perfect property?

Anna: I'm deeply attracted to water, and the same creek that cuts off access was a major selling point for me. I also loved (and love) the remoteness of the land—we can't see any neighbors (except for one light that's visible if you stand in just the right spot in our yard when the leaves are off the trees). As a biologist, I was entranced by the rich woodlands and wetlands—58 acres of them, which is much more than I thought I'd be able to afford!

Mark: I fell in love with the land the first day Anna showed it to me. A life-long dream has been to live somewhere with a nice view and this has 360 degrees of beauty. We have yet to experience the nuisance of a door-to-door salesman.

The Farm on Arrival

Were you nervous or apprehensive about your decision, and if so, why?

Anna: No, I wasn't nervous about buying the land. I get tunnel vision when I really want to do something, and I'd been fixating on this goal for years.

Mark: I was the opposite of nervous—excited and enthusiastic.

What were your intentions? To go off-grid? Become self-sufficient? Escape the rat race? Please elaborate.

Anna: I wanted to live in nature, and have the time to spend there. To me, that meant minimizing my wants drastically so that I could enter the rat race only marginally and on my own terms.

You can see my mission statement written soon after buying the farm, plus my analysis of how close we've come to achieving those initial goals at:

http://www.waldeneffect.org/blog/Eight_years_later/

(That's a year out of date though—we've gotten even closer this year.)

Mark: My intentions were to continue working towards some level of independence and to cultivate some gardening skills and experience.

Did you buy a property with a home/cabin already in place? Why did you make that choice?

Anna: Although there was an old house on the land, my father (who has had extensive building experience) recommended that I tear it down, so I did.

In retrospect, that probably wasn't the best decision. I didn't realize that *he wasn't so much saying the house wasn't structurally sound;* he wanted me to live in something that I now consider posh.

Either way, the house was old and simple enough that it didn't add any value to the property, and that was important to me since I vastly preferred to get more land than to get a house for my very limited money.

Once you tore down the old house, what type of home did you choose? Why did you make that choice?

Anna: We opted to drag a free trailer onto the land after I realized how much time and money it would take to build even a small cabin. Although our trailer does have many downsides (like lack of insulation), it's also an astonishing leap toward independence and simplicity.

Since it was literally worthless, we didn't worry about messing anything up as we learned building skills, and it has kept our taxes low while tempting us to spend more time outdoors. (I write a lot more about this in my upcoming ebook, *Trailersteading.*)

What was the biggest surprise once you made the move? This could either be something funny or something not-so-funny.

Anna: I think the biggest surprise has been how different Mark's and my combined reality is compared to the vision I was aiming for, and how our team-built farm is much better than what I'd originally wanted. For example, in my vision, I would have been hauling buckets of water from the creek to irrigate the garden (because that's what my parents did when I was a kid).

Water System in Action

In our reality, Mark talked me into spending $200 on a pump and another $100 or so on sprinklers to nearly automate the system, which allows us to grow a lot more, higher quality food than we ever could have if we'd been hand-watering.

Compromising and allowing more automation of our lives than I initially felt comfortable with has given us time to research the ecology of our garden systems, which is very satisfying for us, and allows us to avoid even organic pesticides, and is probably better for the environment in the long run.

Mark: I was surprised at how fast the modern world seemed to drift from my attention. There was no T.V. reception and we couldn't afford satellite, so we just quit. That was a major change for me and one of the best health decisions I've made. I substituted satellite radio for a while, but soon felt like it was too mainstream, and I let that go as well.

What is the biggest thing you wish you had done differently right from the beginning?

Anna: I wish I'd found a way to scale back my dreams to a manageable level. We spent a lot of time in the early years biting off more than we could chew and then agonizing over parts of the garden that went to weeds. (Well, I agonized while Mark propped me up.)

I felt that we didn't have the time to take weekends off, but Mark slowly taught me that taking a bit of time off to refresh ourselves actually makes us more efficient overall (plus, time-off is fun).

Mark: We backed Anna's little car up on a rock and scraped a hole in the gas tank. The stuff was dripping fast and we made a quick decision to drive two miles to the local garage and get some mechanical help.

He put it up on the lift so the fuel could drain into a bucket and he started to tell me about these mules he had for sale. "What you really need are some good mules," he suggested, which was a new idea for me.

Long story short is that we were not ready for a team of mules and we may never be (no matter how good of a deal your mechanic makes you).

Has there ever been a time since you made the move that you wished you hadn't? What happened to make you feel this way and how did you deal with these emotions or situations?

Anna: I've only had very momentary lapses of belief in our homestead, generally when I'm feeling overwhelmed. But even then, I didn't want to live anywhere else or in any other way because I realize that I'm happier than anyone else I know. (The only happier person is my husband, who's the one who talks me back to happiness when I slip.)

Mark: I have had zero regrets and when times get a little difficult I just think back to a few of my old jobs and quickly feel lucky to be scraping ice off the composting toilet seat.

Please share information about your property, such as the amount of land you purchased and type of building you live in.

Anna: We have 58 acres, most of which is wooded. We've cleared about a bit more than one acre, which is divided up as I explain at:

> http://www.waldeneffect.org/blog/
> How_much_land_do_we_use_to_grow_
> our_own_food__63__/

We live in a trailer we found for free and then spent $2,000 moving it onto our property.

How much did your life change on a daily routine basis? Did you go from working in an office in a downtown setting to getting up every morning and gardening/chopping wood/ etc...?

Anna: I'd been working online, so my life didn't change that much in that respect. It did take us nine months to get a phone in our remote location, so I did my work from the local library during that period. I'd always spent a lot of time outdoors, but now I channeled that energy into the garden instead of into hiking.

Mark: The biggest change I remember is the deletion of a morning and evening commute. Now I spend that time blogging, or relaxing.

What appliances and other household items did you choose not to have and why? Which ones did you choose to keep and why?

Anna: We pretty much started from scratch, so we made a decision about each appliance as it came time to buy it. We felt like we couldn't live without an electric stove and refrigerator, and soon added a freezer to the mix (since we vastly prefer the flavor of frozen vegetables to canned vegetables).

We don't have a hot water heater or a shower or bathtub or toilet (although we do sometimes consider a point-of-use hot water heater and one of these days we'll install a bathtub and shower, once we've upgraded our living space enough to have a good spot for them). We don't have on-demand treated water—we turn on a little sump pump in the well which pushes water through a sediment filter and a UV light when needed. For washing, we pump water from the creek into a 1,000 gallon tank that gravity feeds into the trailer and then we launder clothes outside with a wringer washer.

We decided not to spend the thousands of dollars to fix the driveway enough that we can drive to our trailer—instead, we walk or use an electric golf cart to ferry supplies if it's dry enough.

Are there any items of furniture/appliances/tools/vehicles that you use that you absolutely would not give up?

Anna: The only really mandatory item is our car—there's no public transportation here and the nearest town isn't really within walking distance. Next are our computers, which allow us to make a living and also to tune into a wider homesteading community. My third favorite appliance is the creek pump, which allows me to irrigate and wash with ease.

Mark: I would add the chainsaw to Anna's list.

What are the most useful items that you use that make your life easier/more enjoyable.

Anna: I adore the trake, which is a high quality trowel which I use for about 80% of my gardening tasks. This year we added porches to the trailer and I think I'd put these on the list too since they give me space to sort the harvest, ferment seeds for saving, and spend much more time outside in the summer. A wheelbarrow in 2011 that's neither too large nor too small really made garden tasks (and firewood, and lots of other things) much easier.

Mark: The most useful item for me would have to be the battery powered drill.

How do you heat your home, power your home, wash clothes, cook, and obtain water?

Anna: We mostly heat with wood, but the little addition we built for Mark is too small and well-insulated to heat with wood unless it's very cold, so he usually uses a space heater there.

We power our home with electricity from the grid; we wash clothes in a wringer washer and dry them on the line, cook on an electric range, and get water in the complex manner I described previously.

We did carry in our drinking water for the first couple of years from a neighbor's spring, which wasn't that tough—just a gallon or two a day between the two of us.

What do you miss from your old life? Please elaborate.

Anna: I used to think I missed luxuriating in a bathtub, but more and more, when I go visit someone and borrow their tub, I find their sterile bathroom not nearly as much fun as soaking in my galvanized washtub in the our summer yard while watching honeybees on the clover. I guess what I really miss most is having close friends at my beck and call in my college dorm, but I left that behind years before heading to the farm.

We're doing better about slowly making good friends close by, and I'm confident I won't even be able to say I miss that in a decade or so.

What is the biggest challenge you faced after making the move?

Anna: Making a living. We live in a very economically depressed region (which is why land prices are so low here), and I didn't want to commute an hour to the nearest city to work. Luckily, we figured out how to market a product to a worldwide audience using the internet (which we explain in our ebook *Microbusiness Independence*). Everything became much easier once we had the money issue figured out and only needed to spend a few hours a week on ensuring our income.

Mark: Of course making a living ends up being the big challenge almost anywhere you choose to hang your hat. I'm happy that jobs were few and far between when we got here. It forced us to think outside the box and come up with a solution ten times better than the best job.

How did you provide food for your family? Did you continue to shop at grocery stores/frequent farmer's markets/barter/grow your own?

Anna: We grow 99% of our vegetables (with the 1% being onions—I never quite grow enough and can't cook without them).

Sweet Potatoes

Our fruit plantings are slower to come into production, but I'd say we're up to providing maybe 20% of our fruit. We buy the rest of our fruit at a local fruit stand (when there's a good selection there—sometimes it's worse than the grocery store) or at the grocery store.

We raise most of our own eggs and white meat (chickens), and buy most of our red meat from a friend who runs a pastured operation. We also have hunted for four deer over the last four years, so that helps.

Anna and Mark's Chickens

We still buy staples at the grocery store—dried beans, flour, sugar, spices, chocolate, etc.

How much of your old life did you leave behind? TV, movies, shopping at the mall, internet, vacations, etc...

Anna: I was never all that keen on mainstream culture, so I didn't really leave that much behind. We do lack TV and radio reception in our holler (Appalachian word for valley), but except for listening to NPR a lot while working, I didn't find that much of a change.

I never took vacations until after we moved to the farm, but even that started to pall a couple of years ago. I mostly prefer to stay home now. The outside world is just so busy and crazy.

Mark: I left it all behind and have never felt better. I still enjoy a good movie, but my tolerance for crappy Hollywood junk has decreased considerably. Unconventional podcasts are a new form of entertainment I've been enjoying.

In your immediate family, who had the most difficult time adjusting and why?

Anna: I guess my immediate family is just me and Mark, and I'd say we each had a tough time adjusting in our own way. I had a hard time adjusting to projects that never got done, while Mark had a hard time adjusting to leaving TV behind.

Mark: It wasn't so much of hard thing to leave TV, but finding healthy substitutes was an adjustment process.

When did you know, with as much certainty as possible, that you had made the right decision?

Anna: I never really doubted the decision to live here, but I can say that I started to feel this astonishing peace I'd never felt before, around 2011.

Mark and I got married in 2008, and that just felt very right. We'd changed our garden over to no-till and were tweaking our system so the produce tasted better with less work.

Our business was booming and for the first time in my life I could buy something beyond the basics (which meant books).

Finally, Mark had trained me to really take the weekends off and to stabilize our work days to 9am - noon then 1 - 4pm, which gave me plenty of time for contemplation and relaxation. We're still in that happy space now.

Mark: I knew the first night we slept in the trailer (that was still missing windows) that this was the best move I had ever made.

If there was ever a time when you felt like you had made the wrong decision, when was it and why did you feel that way?

Anna: I think I most doubted my decision after I'd bought the farm and started trying to whip it into shape, alone, with no budget and minimal tools. It really is a very tough proposition for a single person to start with a briar patch and build a homestead alone, and I'm not sure if I could have done it if Mark hadn't showed up.

Mark: Never have I thought it was the wrong decision.

Did your circle of friends change?

Anna: My closest friends were, and are, buddies from college. However, we spread to the four winds after graduating and some of us have drifted apart, an inevitable occurrence even if I hadn't moved to the farm. On the other hand, I was stunned to realize after buying the farm that there was a whole community of like-minded folks just a mile down the road—they're my parents' age, but otherwise are exactly what I would have wished for. And younger readers of our blog have started to settle somewhat nearby, which is very exciting for us.

What are the greatest rewards you have experienced in your life because of your decision to change your lifestyle?

Anna: I think the inner peace I talked about earlier is the biggest one, which is linked to the amazing bond my husband and I have developed by working together all day, every day.

Runners-up include delicious food, beauty all around me, and time to read and experiment.

Mark: All those things Anna mentioned plus the freedom to do what we want.

Did you experience any issues with building codes/municipal laws that hindered your set-up in regards to building/land use/septic or other permits?

Anna: We just ignored them. When you live a half mile walk through mud from the road, no one cares what you do.

Do you feel that you have gained much more in your life than you gave up? Please explain.

Anna: Definitely. I don't really feel like I gave up anything. Seasonal eating is a good example.

Fresh Strawberries on a Brownie

We started out preserving the summer bounty as fast as possible so we could eat homegrown beans and corn all winter. But we've learned that frost-sweetened kale is actually tastier than even the best summer produce preserved at its peak! So now we mostly just freeze a lot of vegetable soup for the winter and eat out of the garden.

**Kill Mulch
for a New Garden Spot**

We don't miss hot-house cucumbers and tomatoes in December at all because we prefer the taste of the alternatives.

Mark: It's hard to quantify just how much better things are. Giving up most of mainstream culture was a benefit and not a loss.

If there were three pieces of advice that you would give someone considering making this lifestyle change, what would they be?

Anna: Start small. Learn to minimize your wants. Find something you're passionate about.

Mark: I like that list; I'd just move the passion section to number one.

Have you started any new hobbies since you made the move, and if so, how did you discover your newfound interest(s)?

Anna: I started blogging and then writing ebooks after moving in. I'd always liked to write, but never really had the time or sustained attention for it. But when you spend three hours weeding in silence, words just bubble up to the surface.

Mark: I take more pictures, and always seem to have a new subject that excites me—now that we have a bit of free time to explore such things.

How did you make a living prior to your move and what do you do now?

Anna: When I moved to the farm, I was teaching online classes for a local community college and working for an environmental non-profit. While both jobs were much better than the local alternatives, they kept us right at the poverty line and involved a lot of angst.

So when Mark came up with an automatic, POOP-free chicken waterer I was ready to throw my efforts behind the invention and turn it into a cash cow.

---

www.AvianAquaMiser.com

Soon, customers around the world were writing in to tell us how much they loved their waterers! Meanwhile, we also keep a blog where we write about our adventures.

---

www.WaldenEffect.org

I have a slew of ebooks on Amazon and a new paperback, *The Weekend Homesteader*. The combination allows us to make a good living while working only about 10 to 15 hours apiece per week on paid work.

Mark: I had just been laid off from a construction job, and when Anna read Timothy Ferris's book titled *The 4 Hour Work Week* I felt like it was time to branch out on our own.

✳ ✳ ✳

Peace of Mind

Victoria Gazeley

Victoria and her son live in rural British Columbia in an original homesteader's log cabin that her father discovered during a walk in the woods.

Along with her family's help, she dismantled, moved and lovingly restored the cabin where it now rests on six acres of west coast rainforest, providing a piece of paradise for both her and her son to enjoy.

Peace of Mind

*Y*ou know that gut feeling you get when you 'know' that something will happen in your life? That deep down feeling of "YES"!? That's the way Victoria Gazeley felt about her dream of moving to a little homestead on the west coast of Canada. She just 'knew' that was where she was meant to be.

So in 2008, after more than 20 years of living in apartments and townhouses in the city, she packed up her young son and moved into a tiny, family-restored heritage homesteader's cabin a few hundred feet from the ocean, surrounded by hills, hemlocks, and two very noisy ravens.

On her six acres, she's learning how to be more self-sufficient, with a whole lot of simplicity and a big dash of style.

In her work life, she is the owner of a small website design firm, The Cabin Design Studio, helping small businesses build successful, easy to manage websites and graphics that get results.

When she's not working with clients and developing her homestead, you can find her out exploring and traveling with her family and friends, researching and planning her future non-profit organization/foundation, and contributing her many years of communications experience back to her community.

After all those years of city living in apartments and town-houses, she's finally found her place in the woods. And she can't imagine it any other way.

**Victoria's Son
and their
CEO of Egg Laying Operations**

__Making the choice to homestead, live off-grid and/or live in the bush is a life changing decision. What initially led you to make this choice?__

Concern about living in the city during a major disaster (we live in an active seismic zone) or 'power down' situation and the chaos that would ensue was a big driving force. But mostly I simply knew that I was done with city living—we lived near a care facility and a fire hall, so it was sirens 24/7 (which about drove me crazy), plus I just seemed to be on edge all the time, unable to 'wind down'.

It's not that living in the country has *completely* eliminated this (that sort of hard-wiring doesn't just disappear in a couple of years on its own), but it's significantly less noticeable.

To be honest, my original intention wasn't to live 'in the bush'. It was just to get away from the city but we had the cabin available so this is where we ended up.

__Prior to making this decision, were you already familiar with this lifestyle? Were you an outdoor-lover? Farmer or gardener? Hunter? Working at home?__

I grew up in 'the country', but in a subdivision, not on acreage. We spent most of our childhood weekends out in the bush with the family, exploring old logging camps, streams and lakes (my dad worked in forestry and was a long-time outdoorsman – he knew the 'wilds' very well). We learned about what wild plants were edible, how to stay safe from wild animals, and how everything interacted with everything else.

What were your biggest concerns, fears or other factors that you had to consider?

#1 Making a living.
#2 How I'd be able to handle living 'away' from civilization.
#3 If my son would do well living away from other children.

How long was it, from the time you made the decision to the time you actually made the move, and why?

I knew from probably the mid-90s that I would move back to a rural area. I started seriously researching in 2006, and made the move in 2008.

I was living in the city with my son's father at the time, and there was no way he was going to move away from the city where he was born and raised. We weren't doing so well as a couple anyway, so the decision was made.

How did your family react? Please include the reactions of your son as well as extended family if possible.

I was lucky and didn't have any negative reactions, as we moved back to the town where my parents live and not far from where my son's other grandparents live. As for my son, he was only five at the time, so he didn't really understand what was happening, (I don't think).

The fact his father and I made a mutual decision to separate and that he was OK with me moving helped a lot in the whole transition not being so difficult for the little guy.

Your son was very young when you decided to make this move. What was his reaction? Was he excited like many young children might be to begin such an adventure?

I wouldn't say he was excited, but he didn't seem fearful – though he didn't really like the idea of moving to a new school for kindergarten. That wasn't fun for him at all, but we're at the same school still with many of the children he met that first day, so it's all good.

How did you get the process started? For instance, did you need to save money, change jobs, search for property in another area of the province?

Great question. I had been working at the same job for 10 years and approached my boss about the possibility of slowly working myself out of a job. He wasn't happy about it, as we had a long working relationship, but he knew I needed to make the move to stay sane (so to speak... ;)

After a lot of finagling with HR, I was able to work from home two days a week in my full time position, then three days a week, then move to a part-time position for a year before finally leaving altogether to start my own web design and graphics business.

How did you know that you had found the perfect property?

My dad found the old homesteading cabin in the woods near our family's property, and I asked him to show it to me on one of my weekend visits.

You know those moments when you seem to get a 'download' from above, when you just know that there is something you simply have to do? This was one of those moments.

The Original Log Cabin

After making the decision to move the cabin to your family's property, how much work was involved?

The cabin had to be dismantled, moved, dried, and reassembled. It was a labour of love, but one well worth the effort.

Victoria has documented her family's experience restoring her cabin on her blog below. It's well worth reading and may give some of you the inspiration to take on a similar project!

http://modernhomesteading.ca/blog/5-steps-to-moving-and-restoring-a-heritage-log-cabin

Were you nervous about your decision to move to your new home, and if so, why?

Nervous? Not really. I knew it would all work out. But it was definitely a transition, to go from living surrounded by people on all sides to no neighbours for acres. But I always knew it was the right decision.

What were your initial intensions with this move?

I have no intention to go completely off-grid or to drop out of society. My idea was to get to a place where my son could experience rural living, where we could raise some of our own food and we could experiment with self-reliant living, to be able to live less expensively so we could take that money and instead travel or positively impact the lives of others. *I just didn't feel like it was possible in the city.*

How did you handle schooling for your son?

One of the deciding factors for where we ended up was the availability of a Waldorf school nearby. Luckily, my hometown now had one and that's where we ended up. Ultimately, we'll likely end up homeschooling or pooling resources to hire a teacher as our children get older, but for now, the Waldorf school has been the next best thing. There's an elementary school fairly close to our house (the elementary school I attended as a child, actually), but it just doesn't feel 'right' for a sensitive child who loves nature and isn't into the latest pop culture.

What types of activities do you and your son do on a regular basis for entertainment and exercise?

We visit local art shows and events, visit the beach and hang out with friends. Unfortunately, my schedule as the proprietor of a business with international clients keeps me pretty busy (and I love it), so exercise usually takes a back seat. That said, keeping up with the tasks around the property seems to keep things moving... ;)

What types of things does your son do to help around the house or property? Does he embrace this lifestyle as much as you hoped?

It's his job to let the chickens out in the morning, and to secure them at night. He also helps with vacuuming and taking out the compost. He LOVES living here – he's a nature boy at heart and really enjoys the birds and the critters we see here on a daily basis. I knew when he was just a tiny little guy that he'd thrive in a rural setting – thankfully, I was correct... ;)

The Chicken Coup

What are his favorite aspects of your lifestyle?

The chickens, being out in nature, having lots of room to run and explore. Oh, and the frog pond!

Favorite Hen Staking Her Claim on a Pancake

What was the biggest surprise once you made the move?

That we were so busy. When we first moved, I couldn't imagine how we'd fill our days, but quickly they were full – and more...

What was your first Christmas like in your new cabin?

My parents live close by, so we spend Christmas there. I'm hoping though that this year we'll have a tree and spend it here.

Prior to us living here, we'd come to the cabin for Thanksgiving, which was incredibly special. One young friend of the family who is now in her early 20s recently said one of her favorite Thanksgiving memories was the Thanksgiving we all spent here.

What is the biggest thing you wish you had done differently right from the beginning?

Not trying to do so much so quickly. It's discouraging to not get through your 'to-do' list as quickly as you hope to. Baby steps seem to be the key to success when you're doing this on your own.

Has there ever been a time since you made the move that you wished you hadn't? What happened to make you feel this way and how did you deal with these emotions or situations?

Ah... great question. There have been many moments when I wonder out loud what the heck I'm doing here. I think my exact words have been, "I deserve better than this!" when things go sideways or get frustrating.

But then I quickly realize—this is what I wanted all along, and in truth, I love it and honestly wouldn't change a thing.

But in those moments, when the kitchen is too small and things are falling out of the cupboards, or a chicken gets taken by a coyote, or the fire won't light after nine attempts to get it going because there's a low pressure system and the wood got damp, or the satellite internet craps out yet again.........I briefly (very briefly) long for the life when I didn't have to worry about such things, and everything just 'worked'. Except it didn't, really—my life was broken in those days, and while it's not exactly where I want it to be now, it's so much closer than it was.

What helps in those moments is the perspective I get from 'hanging out' with a positive, life-affirming community, both online and off, that speaks life and dreams into me...

A friend put it quite bluntly: "You are living your dream life. What else is there?"

A Slice of Heaven

How much did your life change on a daily routine basis? Did you go from working in an office in a downtown setting to getting up every morning and gardening/chopping wood/ etc...?

HUGE! I went from working in an office full time in the city (regional population 2.5 million) to full time commuting from our new country home, to part-time commuting just one day a week, to working full time for myself from home. Then we added chickens and, well, things REALLY changed! No more zipping off for the weekend at a moment's notice...

What appliances and other household items did you choose not to have and why? Which ones did you choose to keep and why?

Victoria's Kitchen

I have no full size stove, a mini-fridge (we've got a full-size in the shed, but that's fairly recent), and no dishwasher – all 'must haves' when we lived in the city. We make do with a stove-top convection oven, a 2-burner hotplate, a Vitamix, an Omega food processor, and a mini-fridge. I do sort of miss the dishwasher... ;)

Are there any items of furniture/appliances/tools/vehicles that you use that you absolutely would not give up?

Vitamix, Kelly Kettle (for days when the power goes out), hand-crank radio/emergency beacon. And I really do love the little stove-top convection oven. I don't bake (we don't eat much in that realm), so for the two of us, it's been really efficient.

How do you heat your home, power your home, wash clothes, cook, and obtain water?

Our home was heated solely by wood heat (wood stove) until the autumn of 2012. Actually, the main heritage cabin is still heated solely with wood, but when we added a

Woodpiles

small addition in the summer of 2012, the local building code required that we install baseboard heaters in the new rooms, but we don't really use them. We're on our provincial utility for electricity (mostly hydro), and wash our clothes in an old washer we've got up in the well house shed (except for days when it's really nasty; I'm lucky enough to have my parents living nearby and we take our laundry there).

We do have a ceiling-mounted drying rack, and a super-efficient multi-line retractable clothes-line for summer washing, so we do a lot more hand-washing when the season is warmer.

Our water is obtained from a shallow spring-fed well that comes directly off the mountain behind us (luckily, it passes through no other habituated properties – lovely stuff).

Have your cooking habits changed? For instance, do you spend more time cooking now; is your diet healthier; do you eat more fresh food as opposed to your previous diet?

Funny enough, because I'm on my own now with my son, I still cook every night, but it's much simpler fare. With running a business, single parenting, AND ensuring the property, chickens and gardens are kept up, I've discovered I just don't have time to experiment with the culinary skills I used when we lived in the city (put it this way—I used to make homemade pizza—dough included) once a week, Indian food (which takes FOREVER), and regularly tried fancy new recipes. No longer—partly because I don't have the same amount of time, but also because I don't have the same amount of space for food prep... That's been a bit of a challenge.

What is your biggest food craving now that you are farther away from fast food and delivery?

We never got takeout or delivery (well, rarely, anyway), so there's nothing we crave, really.

What do you miss from your old life?

Clean shoes, wearing heels and the occasional dress. Hmmm... that's about it. I really don't miss much at all. We only live an hour from the city via ferry, so if I need a fix, it's easy to get it. Funny enough, I don't do it very often!

What do you absolutely not miss (there are probably many of these)?

Sirens. Loud people in the middle of the night. Traffic. Traffic noise. The constant bombardment with materialism. Advertising everywhere. The frenetic pace.

What is the biggest challenge(s) you faced after making the move?

Being able to ask for help. This is something I've always struggled with – I'm an independent spirit by nature, but I've come to realize that doing this on your own is pretty darned difficult without help. So I'm learning to accept help – and even ask for it sometimes.

What is the biggest reward(s) you have experienced in choosing this lifestyle?

The rewards include the quiet, being able to choose my own schedule, being responsible for my own fate.

But without a doubt one of the greatest rewards is watching the way my son is growing into a very fine young man who loves nature, has a very kind heart, and knows how to create his own fun. This, to me, is priceless.

A Friendly Chick

What benefits do you see your son experiencing that he wouldn't enjoy if he were being raised in a traditional home environment?

Caring for livestock and being responsible for the lives of 20 creatures has taught him responsibility. His love of nature has been nurtured without a lot of effort on my part (short of moving here in the first place, which was not a small feat). His imagination is spectacular, which can be attributed to both not being constantly exposed to mainstream media, TV and the news, and by attending Waldorf School since he was a year old. He appreciates quiet and can find something to do anywhere.

How did you provide food for your family? Did you continue to shop at grocery stores/frequent farmer's markets/barter/grow your own?

We still purchase most of our food at the local organic grocery. I've been so busy getting my business established that I haven't had time to get our food production to the point I thought I would. We do have our own eggs, though, and get raw milk and butter from a local raw milk co-operative.

What do you still buy at the grocery store?

Pretty much everything—except eggs.

Homegrown Eggs

How much of your old life did you leave behind? TV, movies, shopping at the mall, internet, vacations, vehicles; anything you want to add here would be great.

We have no TV, I no longer 'go shopping' for entertainment, and we eat out at restaurants far less than we used to.

When did you know, with as much certainty as possible, that you had made the right decision?

When my son turned to me one day and told me how much he loved living 'in the country'.

Did your circle of friends change? Did you lose friends over this change in your lives, gain new ones?

We've kept a lot of our friends from the city, as they moved out of the city at the same time we did. We've met a lot of new people, but have only become close with a very small handful, mostly because I love just staying home in the evenings!

Cozy Bedroom in the Log Cabin

What are the greatest rewards you have experienced in your life because of your decision to change your lifestyle?

Flexibility in my schedule, the ability to attend my son's school events and volunteer for field trips, etc., and the peace of mind that has come with knowing we're relatively prepared for an extended 'emergency' where we may not have access to all the things we're used to.

If there were three pieces of advice that you would give someone considering making this lifestyle change, what would they be?

Be flexible, know that things won't always turn out how you planned—and that's OK, and don't try to do everything yourself. Ask for help!

Do you feel that you have gained much more in your life than you gave up? Please explain.

Absolutely, without a doubt, for all the reasons mentioned above and more. I always knew I'd leave the city—it just always felt empty to me.

What types of projects have you tackled on your property to help you become more self-sufficient? This could be the addition of a greenhouse, or starting a fish pond – anything.

Greenhouse, raised beds, new fencing, blueberry patch, 20 chickens, emergency food stores, wild-crafting, learning how to preserve food.

Do you think that you will continue living this way for the rest of your life? Could you ever see yourself living in the city or suburbs again?

I can, but with more resources at my disposal, and maybe with someone else looking after the livestock on a day to day basis. But live in the city again—I just don't see it happening.

Where has the biggest source of information come from — books, internet, or other people who made this move prior to yours?

Internet research, my mentor Robin Wheeler, who we unfortunately lost in February of 2012, and my amazing Facebook page friends at facebook.com/modernhomesteading.

For those who wish to read more about Victoria and her son's experiences visit:

Modern Homesteading

http://www.modernhomesteading.ca

on Facebook

http://www.facebook.com/modernhomesteading

Victoria's Business

http://www.thecabindesignstudio.com

Email

victoria@modernhomesteading.ca

Voice From the Bush

Linda Roberts & Charlie Johnson

Linda and Charlie live in a cozy, single-story board and batten home on a forty-acre mining claim. Surrounded by rocks and trees in Northern Ontario they have found the life they dreamed of, amidst the peace and quiet of the bush.

Voice From the Bush

*L*inda (Little Bear) and Charlie (Charlie from the Bush) have been living off the grid for over ten years now and in that time they have had several medical emergencies, survived wild animal and nasty human attacks, learned to feed themselves (for the most part) and helped to change laws.

Linda and Charlie met at a 12- step program that frowns on moving to solve ones problems, but in this case it looked like a great plan!

So they loaded up the truck and moved north, to the little claybelt area, past North Bay and far from the city lights. Their move proved to be a jumping-off point to a remote forty acres of rocks and trees on an abandoned mining claim in the Silver Center area of Temiskaming.

Making the choice to homestead/live off-grid/live in the bush is a life changing decision. What initially led you to make this choice?

Charlie: We had moved to the near north to find a healthier and more respectful way of living. Our time as urban professionals had left us both feeling ill, exhausted and spiritually bereft. After major substance abuse (Linda), mental health meltdowns (me) and culture fatigue (˜!) we both had found 12-step programs, psychotherapy and creative outlets. We thought the north might provide a further step in our ongoing search for spiritual growth.

We moved north but found 'town' was still not far enough away so we purchased a property well off the beaten path. Like many folks we thought that 'one day' we might consider using it for more than an occasional retreat.

Linda: A faulty heater, subsequent court case and further utility nightmares found us moving the date up! With a small inheritance we designed and built our little home and have lived here since 2002.

There were some obvious clues as to what to do and where to move that we both recognized as guidance from outside of our experience. People, situations and lots of birds enter into the guidance experience but we'll leave it at that rather than sound extremely flakey! We are flakey, just not in the extreme.

Prior to making this decision, were you outdoor-lovers? Farmers or gardeners? Hunters? Working at home? Campers?

Charlie: I always explored ways of gardening, growing the family's vegetables in Southern Ontario and my *then* wife and family had goats, rabbits and chickens. Although I butchered the rabbits, I wasn't so good at the larger animals. I would collect fresh road kill more out of curiosity than any desire for self-sufficiency and wild plant foods formed part of this curiosity.

Some twenty years ago, I started an interest in wild medicinal plants that has stood me in very good stead when dealing with various aches and pains. This started by having to deal with the side effects of my psychiatric medications and has led me to make some wonderful creams.

I've found that one herb book alone is likely unreliable, so have three or four reference books. The best is *The Complete Herbal Handbook for Farm and Stable* by Juliette de Bairacli Levy, followed by *Culpeper's Color Herbal* edited by David Potterton, then *Indian Herbalogy of North America* by Alma R. Hutchens. Euell Gibbons' books are also very good.

Linda: I grew up in the near north and spent my childhood with my grandmother in Muskoka. I led a very urban life in adulthood but remembered my childhood with Nana as a wonderful time and had always said that I wanted to 'paint and colour and live in the woods'.

I am living my childhood dream.

What were your biggest concerns, fears or other factors that you had to consider?

Charlie: My biggest concern was to get away from western society, as far away as I could. The last night I spent in town, I was screaming at the neighbours, screaming at the T.V. And when I started screaming at Linda, she said: "Take the dogs and a lot of your breakfast cereal and go to the house in the bush. I'll drive out in the morning to see if there's anything you need. Just go."

That first winter, apart from the endless work where

Linda and Charlie's Summer Kitchen

the learning curve felt like it was vertical for the first three years or so, our biggest problem was the fire in our air-tight wood cookstove (top of the line, thank you Linda). We were terrified of letting it go out, so we'd burned ten of our twelve cords of wood by Christmas. We were saved from having to give up by a Christmas present of three cords of wet firewood, which was even hauled up the driveway (300 yards) for us. We dried logs all over the house as we struggled with how to light the fire.

Linda: I was not concerned or afraid. I am a recovered heroin addict so the concept of having to learn new ways was nothing compared to my learning curve in my decade as a junkie. I was an overachiever so had almost always worked while addicted and this way of life was also tough but in a very different way.

The first winter was hard on me in terms of cleaning! I was a real neat and tidy person and had to learn how to live within very different boundaries. An elder friend told me the secret of town clothes/home clothes and work clothes, which is how I arrange things now and has it ever saved on laundry!

There are other things the farm women taught me and I learned to go to the local elder care facility for advice and suggestions. We have done ourselves a great disservice by corralling our old people and hiding them away from us and our youth. They are there with so many answers and nearly nobody asking the questions.

Practical concerns that held importance for me have evolved, usually with me relaxing my standards! If I think back the biggest worry I had was how I would handle the lack of contact with others.

How long was it, from the time you made the decision to the time you actually made the move, and why?

Charlie: We decided to leave Hamilton about three months before actually leaving, and left mainly because of the deteriorating social conditions outside our door in the east end—things like automatic small-arms fire in the street at night. Once we arrived in Haileybury, we realised that we hadn't gone far enough and stumbled (God-directed better) onto an old silver mining claim that had been for sale for a long time.

Linda: Within two and a half years of leaving Hamilton (that decision to move eight hours up the highway took only a couple of months to implement) we were out here supervising the foundation work. We moved to get away from a culture that was not working out for either of us.

Imagine doing all the therapy and making all the changes to learn to live in *21st Century Canada* only to realize that the culture itself is dramatically flawed. That was the central reason for our move. Everything was breaking down; Toronto, the biggest city in Ontario was still putting its raw sewage into Lake Ontario. When people in Hamilton complained about their drinking-water I suggested they fill their bathtubs with water; drink out of one end and poop into the other then see how long it worked for them.

How did your family react? Please include the reactions of immediate family as well as extended family if possible.

Charlie: I have no idea how my family felt as we're not very close and when we are, we tend to be highly competitive.

Linda: My family was just glad I wasn't in prison or stoned! My father was worried but both my sisters had led alternative lifestyles (one on a boat on the West Coast and the other on Vancouver Island off the grid) so weren't worried. My mother was thrilled for me. She always had total confidence that I could do anything.

How did you get the process started? For instance, did you need to save money, change jobs, search for property in another area of the country or buy property in another country?

Charlie: My parents died, shortly after we'd arrived in Haileybury. I discovered that my share of their estate was enough to buy the property and build the shell.

We finished the inside on credit cards, which we maxed. We didn't care about having a zero credit rating as we operate on the philosophy of having an "identity" that nobody wants to steal anyway, in other words as close to a cash economy as we can arrange.

Linda: We were able to buy the land from a woman who had just been fired from her job and needed the cash.

We finished on credit. We contacted the creditors and told them we were broke and wouldn't be paying them back. Most of them took it very well.

How did you know that you had found the perfect property?

Charlie: We were told so by a raven who is the Messenger. Subsequent reasoning showed that further north had serious problems, as did further south.

We live on a gravel road that only goes to a hydro dam, basically a road that goes nowhere. This suits us with our anti-Western culture lifestyle.

Linda: We heard about the owner of the property and called her the day she lost her job. We have great plowing and maintenance service on our road due to the dam (irony) and, as I mentioned earlier, the birds play a big part.

One day, as I traveled back and forth with supplies, my passenger, a woman in early recovery asked, "What are those big birds flying beside the car every day?" They were golden eagles. They flew me in and out of the valley for the four months we were building. It is easy to know when and how and what I am supposed to do these days!

Were you nervous about your decision, and if so, why?

Charlie: No, I wasn't, because I knew very well that I couldn't tolerate town any more. Linda wondered if we were tough enough and flexible enough to make a go of it.

Her questions were answered when I bushed our truck nineteen kilometres away from the nearest house and we had to walk out. She had to trust that I would go on alone when she couldn't go any further and I had to find reservoirs of strength that I never knew I had to make it to a house, then find the courage to knock on the door of a perfect stranger to ask them to save our lives in the middle of the night.

Linda: I found out, before we made the decision to build, that in the middle of winter, in 15 below temperatures, we could reverse roles and get out alive. Turning on a dime, problem solving without ego or self-deception and, most of all, trust in each other are the traits I saw we had so I was no longer nervous. In February we had our true test—compliments of the forest—and we passed with flying colours. In May we began building. In August we moved out to the bush.

That night, as I sat in the little igloo I carved out of the snow bank, I sang with the rocks and the trees and the stars. I am part of this place. I was quite ready to let the body go and take up the song in earnest. Still am.

What were your intentions? To go off-grid? Become completely self-sufficient? Escape the rat race?

Charlie: Get away from western culture.

Linda: To have ourselves to depend on, rather than the un-trustworthy utility companies and food-sellers. To go off-grid, to be as self-sufficient as possible and primarily to get away from the "money first" culture that is dreadful and just plain rude to us all. As I write this, the largest recall of food in the history of humans is ongoing. Poop in the food. Yummy.

Did you build a home/cabin? Why did you make that choice?

Charlie: We built a 500 square foot, one bedroom house with a 250 square foot shop attached (where the water system and other equipment is stored/used).

Inside Linda and Charlie's Home

Linda: We wanted to be sure that the insulation was thick and that the position of the home in relation to the prevailing winds was right. We wanted to have a home that looked like it belonged in the woods while keeping it easy to heat and within our design abilities!

What was the biggest surprise once you made the move? This could either be something funny or something not-so-funny.

Charlie: We are so far out that we are the law out here. The emergency services etc. are half an hour away after they've been effectively contacted. For example, when I bushed the truck I called the Ontario Provincial Police to let them know. It was a Saturday, so the local detachment was closed for the weekend. The call centre had no idea where I was talking about and when I was asked, "Are you anywhere near Groom Drive?" I thanked them and hung up because their nearest reference point was forty kilometers away!

Our biggest surprise was the number and seriousness of the law-breakers that roam around here. Gun-toting hunters who will shoot anything day or night, legal or not, are commonplace. We were really bothered by what to do about this until a neighbour explained that the boundary of our property is where our concern stops. Inside this line, we fight to the death. Outside, not our problem. Linda was able to negotiate this effectively with gun-toting Americans when their campers were shooting up our property.

Linda: The AA book says our experience can be beneficial someday. So talking to hoods and crooks and poachers has been effective, thanks to my past. I have been surprised however. The local conservation officers asked me to let them know when I became aware of poaching. I told them I'd be happy to help as soon as I got my badge, gun, Kevlar vest and first paycheque. I am not the law. We have even been asked to 'eat the evidence' after a hunter's successful partridge hunt.

What is the biggest thing you wish you had done differently right from the beginning?

Charlie: Learned the importance of having lots of dry kindling always available, especially for the winter.

Linda: Learned how to manage a proper fire! The first year it was like a sauna in here. The butter turned to ghee. Santa brought us some wood that year. These days we are much better fire-keepers.

Has there ever been a time since you made the move that you wished you hadn't? What happened to make you feel this way and how did you deal with these emotions or situations?

Charlie: My commitment to our way of life is reinforced every time I return from town. I have absolutely no regrets.

Linda: I have no regrets. I am happier than I ever thought possible, especially the unexpected peace of mind I have developed after being able to grow and forage good food. When I learned how to collect, make viable and store my own seeds I felt a calm spot in the center of my being. Very unexpected. Wonderful feeling. It's still here.

Please share some of the details of your property.

Charlie: We bought a forty-acre mining claim that's basically rocks and trees and have added several out-buildings for chickens, now gone, and rabbits, also now gone, and most importantly for storage of all those important, you-never-know things.

Linda: We live in a single-story home with rough sawn lumber board-and-batten exterior, a deck and summer kitchen on the front and a shop with important storage areas for water and grains, etc. The inside is very cozy and built to suit us very well. Work areas and storage areas are well thought out for the most part. Our floors are very high quality fake ceramic. After 10 years it is still going strong, as are the counter tops. I broke the 'sale' box of ceramic tiles into patterns on the three countertops for a total of $100.00. I hope to replace one area with a wooden slab when we find the right piece of wood! We have a double-gauge steel roof with Gyproc panels underneath, both for sound cushioning and for a heat-break in the event of fire.

How much did your life change on a daily routine basis? Did you go from working in an office in a downtown setting to getting up every morning and gardening/chopping wood/ etc...?

Charlie: Our way of life changed completely. The loss of outside electricity cut down the creative time in the day from six to eight hours a day, to maybe two if I'm lucky. Otherwise, I comfort myself by thinking how much I would be earning if a professional was doing what I was right then. E.g. When doing plumbing work, I pretend I'm making seventy bucks an hour. This keeps me going when I ask myself why I do this.

Linda: Everything changed. We went totally cold-turkey (again, my usual method of change!) and have added a few things recently. The satellite internet and the cell tower have helped us communicate. The phone isn't used much but is primarily a safety device now that we are older.

What appliances and other household items did you choose not to have and why? Which ones did you choose to keep and why?

Charlie: No fridge; it's not needed in winter, replaced with good coolers and ice blocks in summer. No TV because we didn't have the hydro to run it; also I hate it. Linda insisted on the best all-night wood cook stove that money could buy. It's a GEM.

Linda: No electricity. No items with plugs. We bought a 100 year old washer and a 2002 replica white enamel and chrome wood cook stove with airtight system. It is our only source of heat in the house. It is all we need. In summer perishables are kept in a cooler in the cool shop. Our neighbour (about 8 km away) sells ice all summer to the tourists so we use ice when needed.

Are there any items of furniture/appliances/tools/vehicles that you use that you absolutely would not give up?

Charlie: The pick-up truck, my buck saws, my five-pound splitting axe, my German hand-grinder for our flour.

Linda: The wood stove, the Jeep (less snow shoveling), the water purifier and the raised garden beds. The pressure canner is absolutely vital. We preserve all spring, summer and fall so we have over 600 jars of safe, local, delicious food each year.

Fresh Produce!

How do you heat your home, power your home, wash clothes, cook, and obtain water?

Charlie: Wood heat, with kerosene lanterns for additional heat in the outer plumbing shed, also for most light. We run our computers from a very small gas generator or several solar panels.

We cook on a propane two-burner stove in the summer or a summer-kitchen wood cook stove; we wash at the laundromat in town, or occasionally in a hand-powered washer, in summer.

Because all the ground water around here is seriously contaminated with arsenic released by the silver mining, we collect the water from the roof, stored in a 1500 U.S. gallon tank. Drinking water is from a Water Tiger sand filter, obtained from them online in Victoria, B.C. This water is of excellent quality.

What do you miss from your old life? Please elaborate.

Charlie: Nothing.

Linda: Nothing. Elaborate...ok, I don't miss the phone company lying to me, the gas leaking from the inferior heating unit, the outside eating area next door with its midnight sounds of teenagers making out, the phone ringing, someone at the door when least wanted, the town digging up the road *and our lawn* in front of the house for no apparent reason, the increased municipal taxes, etc ...

Oh, wait, I do miss something! Ice cream!
But I only have to drive to town for it.

What is the biggest challenge you faced after making the move?

Charlie: Learning this new way of life.

Linda: Learning to let go of certain things. For example, the two dogs bring in sand. So I realized that sand was actually wearing the dirt off the floor (like a nice apricot facial rub exfoliates one's skin) so am good about the floor now. Less washing seems to have been good for the flooring, too! My biggest challenge was learning to let go of driving to town to share what I've learned. Too hard to bring the bush to town so I have found other ways that are less taxing, like websites and children's books.

How did you provide food for your family? Did you continue to shop at grocery stores/frequent farmer's markets/barter/grow your own? Please specify for both produce and meat/fish.

Linda: We grow lots, forage some and buy from our farmer friends in season. Preserving is done by drying, pressure canning, dry canning and smoking.

How much of your old life did you leave behind? TV, movies, shopping at the mall, internet, vacations, vehicles; anything you want to add here would be great.

Charlie: We left them all for the first seven years except the vehicle. Now we've added the satellite link and our own cell tower. We plug them in to our batteries when we feel the need.

When did you know, with as much certainty as possible, that you had made the right decision?

Charlie: As soon as I moved out here.
Linda: Right away!

If there was ever a time when you felt like you had made the wrong decision, when was it and why did you feel that way?

Charlie and Linda: Never

Did your circle of friends change? Did you lose friends over this change in your lives, gain new ones? Please elaborate.

Charlie: I was well used to this, since I'd emigrated from England, quit a salaried position to start a new life, before even thinking of coming north.

What are the greatest rewards you have experienced in your life because of your decision to change your lifestyle?

Charlie: Freedom and mandatory physical exercise.

What are the biggest challenges you have faced?

Charlie: An attempted take-over of our property by some sicko drug dealers. This caused me to start writing our "From the Bush" newsletter. It is still being published with local ads for financial support and is highly appreciated by my community.

Linda: There were prospectors who were really grow-op people and tried to terrorize us into leaving. We did fine.

We don't scare easy after prison and the loony bin. I am really sure they had no idea about our pasts so they thought we'd leave.

Instead I used them to change mining law!

In 2009 the Mining Act was changed to include foraging for food/fruit to eat or sell and for herbs/medicines for personal health; this trumped the rights of the people of Canada to exploit minerals under that ground.

Surface rights won out and the 2012 Mining Act reflects even more changes including the rights up north to be taken off the Claim Map due to lifestyle.

As a woman of aboriginal descent, I am happy to see
that the direction my moccasins walk
counts more than lost paperwork from a century ago!

We were the first people to file for the newly created document in 2012! We set a high bar for future applicants.

As residents it is a Sacred Trust to speak on behalf
of residents without voices.

Our advocacy has changed mining law but also prevented poisonous defoliant 'release xrt" from being helicopter sprayed over the forestry management area.

We have helped children build raised beds and make gardens in three local towns. In our third year of expansion the gardens got provincial funding via the 'Best Start' program so children at daycares throughout Ontario can eat some food they grow themselves!

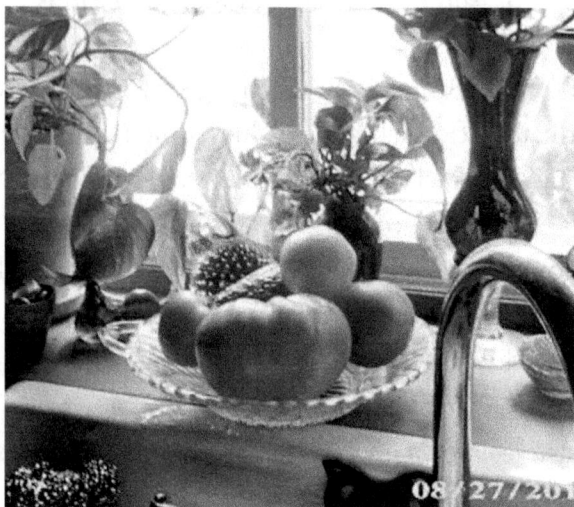

Fresh Produce in the Window

If there were three pieces of advice that you would give someone considering making this lifestyle change, what would they be?

Charlie: 1) Do it while you're young! I was sixty; had I waited any longer I would have been too old to catch up physically.

2) Have some sort of reliable income so you can keep up the strenuous effort required to succeed off-grid.

3) Building from scratch is easier than taking over the problems of an old home.

Linda: 1)Fix up one spot to look at that is finished so you can stay focused on what you want.

2) Write a poster of why you are doing it so you can stay focused on the goals.

3) Have a separate set of clothes for physical work/home living/town outings (this info from a farm wife to whom I was complaining about my laundry). The first two categories need far less laundering! It's the reason all those photos of pioneer women show them in starched white aprons...they got the clean one out for the photo-op....and they aren't smiling either...'cause they were tired.

Do you feel that you have gained much more in your life than you gave up? Please explain.

Charlie: Yes. I have a life, instead of a slow death in a hostile culture.

Linda: I have learned the true value of playing in the woods. It only took 50 years to get here!

Have you started any new hobbies since you made the move, and if so, how did you discover your newfound interest(s)?

Charlie: Writing. Also, I've recently started painting pictures again.

Linda: Illustrating children's books with stories from our newsletters. Our life here results in many stories.

We will never run out of ideas for books.

"Charlie from the Bush" is a local character known and loved by our whole community. We are home.

Charlie from the Bush and his Smoker

How did you make a living prior to your move and what do you do now?

Charlie: After training and working as an engineer I became a psychiatric patient for twenty years and was living on a small disability pension. On reaching 65 this pension was doubled with my Old Age Pension/CPP/GIS.

Linda has started a web design and management business that's going well. We are also publishing a series of children's books based on the experiences that we have had out here. The first of these is *Charlie from the Bush and the Hungry Bear.*

Linda: After years of big city living, in Montreal and Toronto, working for clothing designers, printers, freelancing artwork and being a drug addict, my most recent 21 years of sobriety have been filled with creativity of all kinds.

I am a painter whose paintings are all sold; a children's book illustrator and publisher (whose books sell themselves) and a maker of medicine objects for people from all over the world.

For cash and barter: I design and manage websites for area businesses.

For empowerment: I teach women with basement businesses to design and manage their own websites.

For love: I create beadwork with natural objects and Japanese glass beads called 'delicas'.

For respect: I advocate for trees, rocks, animals and marginalized people in need of help.

Linda 'Little Bear'

My previous business was creating beaded fur and moose hide mocs, mitts, hats and bags but I became chemically sensitive and allergic to tanning chemicals, especially chromium. With commercial tanning so polluting it was time for me to stop supporting it anyway.

I am still able to work with traditional tanned hides and black tanned hides.

Please also include anything else that you feel you would like to share with readers. We appreciate any information you wish to include.

Linda: Charlie and I tried our best to fit in to the 20th century urban mosaic. We both got jobs and families and cars and homes and it didn't work. We tried to medicate our way through until that became the problem. We met at AA and, finding a place that helped guide us to some self-respect, we kept looking at the next respectful thing to do.

It became obvious that we were taking way more than we were giving in the city, then in the town, and finally we realized we had to create an environment that felt honorable. It was a lot of work to build and furnish and fit our home out for simple, organized living and we did it. We have no idea how.

Grace is the most likely answer.

Help came from all over the place—from two guys willing to brave the bush in fly season, and friends showing up with drums and flutes on my first birthday in the bush, to Joe Milroy, (since moved on to the Blue Road of Spirit), who showed up our first Christmas with a bushel basket full of groceries, to our tow guy Jim, who arrives in the middle of nowhere and giggles through whatever wacky situation we get into.

New Year's Day, 2013, he pulled the jeep out of the ditch...again. Today we honour our environment by re-using things that were already made; we repair and mend, pass on that which we no longer need to those who appreciate it and we spend time considering what we do.

We vote with our loony and try to support our local businesses even if things are cheaper elsewhere, we share what we are learning and we interact in a meaningful way with others. We are well-known, and people, on occasion, seek us out as wise friends who will answer questions and keep the conversations private. We still fire up the little generator when there isn't enough solar for our internet and we still shop at Walmart and eat in restaurants.

But we come home to "Charlie & Linda Land"
where the trees and the rocks and the stars greet us;
it makes us weep for the sheer beauty of it All.

We have many projects including: Charlie creating Appalachian Mountain Dulcimers for those who need the vibrations of music, his oil paintings of the memories of flowers long since wilted away, and his "Charlie from the Bush" monthly newsletters on topical issues in our community and the world.

I continue to make what I call 'visual aids' to help us stay focused on our goals and on being the people we aspire to be. I paint and publish the "Charlie from the Bush" children's picture book series available at:

www.charliefromthebush.com

I bead beautiful items for the local spring Rock Show and run my own small business "Voice from the Bush", a communication technology firm specializing in web design, marketing and publishing.

Our website has free downloads of other books, stories and recipes. We have lots of photos with a more focused look at the nuts and bolts planned for spring viewing.

www.voicefromthebush.com

Every year I give a talk to the Wilderness Rescue Graduates at our local Veterinary College and I tell them their lives will be unlike most other peoples'. They can expect to be underpaid, under-appreciated and, when successful, the creature they helped to save will leave, breaking their hearts and making them feel full with the experience of putting something right.

That would be my wish for everyone: Feeling Fulfilled...or as they say in AA; "Happily and Usefully Whole".

✳✳✳

Adventures at Coösauke

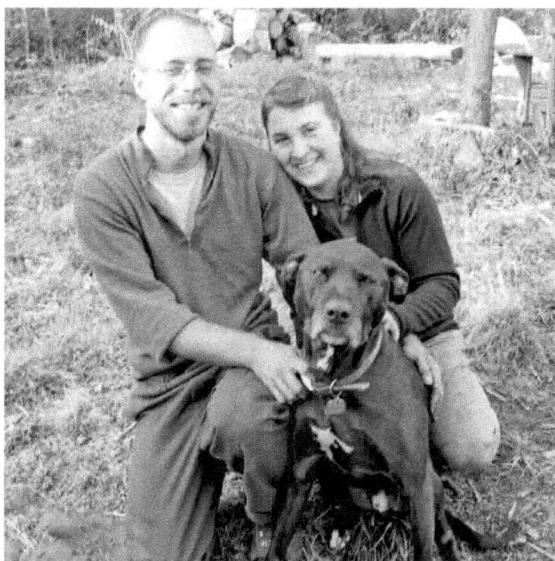

Bethann A. Weick & Ryan J. Harvey

Bethann, Ryan and their pooch Mica live on more than 28 acres located on the south branch of the Baker River in Dorchester, NH.

Coösauke, meaning "Place of the Pines", consists of a river, wooded hillside, springs, mixed hardwood forest, original yurt, and a new 16x18 log cabin that they constructed from trees harvested from their own property.

Adventures at Coösauke

$\mathcal{B}$ethann A. Weick is a writer, gardener, and homesteader living in Dorchester, NH. Originally hailing from Kintnersville, PA, the daughter of a farrier and a gardener/activist, Beth graduated from Colgate University (Hamilton, NY) with a degree in Latin American Studies and Social Geography.

Having lived in Spain, the Dominican Republic, Peru, and Mexico, Beth's most formative experiences were in the White Mountains of New Hampshire. Here she worked nine seasons for the Appalachian Mountain Club in backcountry huts and shelters. Backcountry skills, stewardship ethics, and a penchant for simplicity were honed in these years.

A love of the mountain landscape, merged with a passion for

rural life, led Beth to Dorchester, NH. Moving to the area in 2008, she spent four years working and living at D Acres Farm & Educational Homestead. Small-scale no-till agriculture, animal husbandry, and rustic living accommodations, as well as community outreach and educational initiatives, defined this experience.

In 2012, she has joined her partner Ryan at Coösauke and now works as a writer/editor, as well as performing garden consultation, design, and maintenance services. She volunteers with the Museum of the White Mountains, the Old Hutsman Association, and the Dorchester Cemetery Committee.

Ryan J. Harvey is a forester, trails foreman, EMT, and homesteader. Ryan grew up in the Berkshires of western Massachusetts and graduated from Paul Smith's College with an A.A. in Environmental Studies and a B.S. in Natural Resources; Management and Policy.

He has served under many capacities within public land management throughout the northeastern mountains specifically the Adirondacks and the White Mountains.

From 2004 to the present Ryan has served as the trails foreman of the Pemigewasset District of the White Mountain National Forest. Outside of public land management Ryan works as a consulting forester and in other capacities of land management.

He remains passionate and active in the international Shambhala-Buddhist community. Ryan settled in the Baker River Valley of New Hampshire, venturing initially with his former wife in homesteading and living "off the grid" in an intentional community, a small organic farm, and then living in their hand built yurt for five years until settling onto Coosauke. Ryan remains active as a local volunteer EMT, Chairman of Dorchester's Conservation Commission, and Executive Council Member of the White River Shambhala Center.

Making the choice to homestead/live off-grid/live in the bush is a life changing decision. What initially led you to make this choice?

For both Ryan and I, we arrived at homesteading through a gradual process of life experiences and perspectives. It has not been a singular decision that we can trace to a particular time or event. For both of us, it is the more conventional lifestyle that would require such a defined decision.

Prior to making this decision, were you already familiar with this lifestyle? Were you outdoor-lovers? Farmers or gardeners? Hunters? Working at home? Campers?

Ryan: No, I was not familiar with this lifestyle. However, I spent most of my childhood in the woods, often solitary. I always went to the mountains or woods for solace. Any familiarity was through my grandmother, who shared stories of working on her family homestead farm.

Beth: Not to the extent that we are living now – i.e. I grew up with power, running water, standard conveniences. However, I also grew up with a garden, animals and parents who encouraged free-thinking and the pursuit of self-sufficiency. The mountains and the value of being outdoors were significant influences. Prior to joining Ryan at Coösauke, I worked as a farmer for years, gaining skills and familiarity in this manner.

What were your biggest concerns, fears or other factors that you had to consider?

Ryan: My fears are not obligated to my lifestyle—my fears are the same regardless of daily choices. That being said, my most significant fear is of losing the physical ability to do the things I want to do, in particular because I've designed a life so hinged on being strong and physically capable. There's so much pride that comes with that—and the loss of that would be devastating.

Beth: At the outset I feared losing social connections. Post college, I chose to have no phone, no car, no email—letters (and walking) were my only means of reaching those I was not immediately living with. Would this be enough? I was fearful that I would have to "return"—so to speak—to a more modern means of connecting with people.

For both of us, too, there was the fear of burning bridges with the conventional/modern world—university degrees, academic skills, job experiences, etc. In our own way we each diverged from the track these skills put us on in favor of living the ideals we each held. Each time this decision is reinforced, the implication is that it would—will—be harder to return to such a mainstream pattern if we needed to. This continually implies the questions: "Can I support myself? Can I sustain what I believe is right, or best?"

How long was it, from the time you made the decision to the time you actually made the move, and why?

Beth: Again, this was a gradual process. My childhood instilled me with ideas and basic skills (my parents were a horse-shoer and a gardener). The post-college years were the first time I felt free to choose completely for myself and I choose a path less than conventional. This led to employment in the backcountry, then to farming, and eventually to our homestead (at age 27). It is hard to separate a beginning and end from this trajectory, even in hindsight.

Ryan: The process began early in my time at college where I was focused on woods work and self-sufficiency. This was coupled with working in many capacities in backcountry and wilderness stewardship positions. Through hiking and climbing and that community I began to realize that I didn't need as much as I thought. I wanted to blend the two together instead of living a dualistic life.

I was also greatly influenced by my grandmother who loved to share stories of the yesteryears about farming and the old ways. It wasn't until I moved here (the north country of NH) and stumbled upon a community where I felt like I could live forever that I at some point—deliberate or uncon-scious—decided to stay. So it was only natural that I would look and search for an ideal piece of property.

A Snapshot of Beth and Ryan's Property

How did your family react? Please include the reactions of immediate family as well as extended family if possible.

Ryan: I believe my immediate family was supportive, initially, with the idea perhaps that this was just a phase. At some point they began to realize I was serious, and began to question my decisions. It has taken years, but now they genuinely support my endeavors, and at times seem to be quite proud of them. Outside of my immediate family, people were very supportive, and at times almost held me to the regard of some iconic figure—a position I always felt awkward to be in.

Beth: My immediate family is very supportive. My parents maintain great enthusiasm for the life I am living—it was them, after all, who set me on this path. They have recently moved up to Dorchester, and are physically supportive of our homestead work as well as emotionally enthusiastic for what I, and we, are doing. My extended family however, finds my choices foreign and unimaginable—romantic concepts, perhaps, but not understandable.

I remain a curiosity; my joy and the presence of a partner to share in this with, tempers such sentiments a bit. If love and happiness is understood, however, the situation in which I am finding it is not.

How did you get the process started? For instance, did you need to save money, change jobs, search for property in another area of the country or buy property in another country?

Beth: Frugality has been a habit all my life—not sure how or why I learned this, but it is ingrained. For me, preparation was mental as much as physical. I spent my early 20s simplifying my mental processes, mental needs, understanding how to sync my mind/body to a better extent. I feel like this has afforded me a grounded personality and perspective to steadily pursue a life, not just a living. Cultivating a sense of stewardship, holism in life choices, these were the first steps. The acquisition of practical skills has been ongoing since childhood. I have been lucky in that settling into a relationship, I have also settled onto land.

Ryan: My former wife and I did save money for years for a down payment on a piece of land. Our search lasted for about three years. We had very specific demands on a property which had really paired down our choices, including remoteness and ease of access to town. Our jobs were seasonal in the arena of forestry, trail work, and farming. In those aspects we were already well familiar with what was at hand (regarding skills). Before moving to Coösauke, I have always lived in rustic situations, i.e. off-grid cabins, a local small farm, and a yurt. For those five years, I never had running water, electricity, and/or modern conveniences, so my habits were already there.

How did you know that you had found the perfect property?

Ryan: Finding the property, Coösauke, was very auspicious. It was the first property we seriously looked at for purchase and at the time was priced very high. I couldn't afford it. For three years we searched and could not find a property that reflected a somewhat ideal set-up for a large garden, water, cabin, sugar bush, southern exposure, and a sense of wildness.

When the property dropped substantially in price we were alerted by a friend/broker, and immediately visited the property again. We literally signed the paperwork *that day* on the roof of his car. It may not be the most ideal property for a homestead in the conventional sense, but it has wildness, history, a good wood-lot, a sugar bush, good ground for gardening, river frontage, and great exposure to south/southwest. It is a perfect piece of property that brings the mountains home.

Were you nervous about your decision, and if so, why?

Ryan: I wasn't really nervous about the decision as we had been looking for some time. We were more nervous about how we would live for a few months afterward as we drained our bank accounts entirely to make the initial down payment on the property.

Beth: Joining Ryan at Coösauke came at the culmination of other endeavours—primarily my involvement with a farm/community nearby. Rather than nervousness, there was a sense of anticipation and excitement.

What were your intentions? To go off-grid? Become self-sufficient? Escape the rat race? Please elaborate.

Beth: My ideals have been a self-sufficient, sustainable, quiet life, lived in the woods. I have wanted to live in rhythm with the seasons, and define my endeavors by the natural patterns that surround me. Ultimately, I have strived to live the lessons learned in the backcountry of the White Mountains (NH).

Mountains, for me, represent dramatic weather and a harsh landscape–both of which are a stark background for life lessons of humility, vulnerability, life/death, as well as lessons in simplicity and the redefinition of needs. Mountains, however, can't be lived in for a lifetime; they are a landscape which can be passed through, learned from, but not lived in. Homesteading is a means of integrating the mountains into a daily existence.

By homesteading, I am able to pursue ethics of providing for myself, living simply and lightly on the land. In this, too, is much joy. In eliminating the frivolities and flashy distractions of contemporary society, I have chosen a life with roots, and with contentment based in place not in consumption.

Ryan: My intentions were to live and be in touch with raw existence. Ultimately, I want to live a life that is un-fabricated and to see reality as it is, to have the opportunity to do so. Also I want to live with a piece of land intimately for the rest of my life, learning the intricacies of the seasons, etc. With that said, I have chosen to have a certain element of self-sufficiency and utility present, as well as artistry and creativity. I have identified these as conduits to live my ideals. I have tried not to be too harsh with respect to how much of this or that I am independent of–I see this to be no different from the competition of the conventional modern world. Thus, I try to continually combine an element of self-sufficiency and community.

Did you buy a property with a home/cabin already in place?

No. We wanted a somewhat remote and isolated property so that ruled out a lot of properties with homes already on them.

Also, we had to get a loan for the property and we did not want to feel confined to the banks wants and wishes in terms of building standards, etc.

Did you build a home/cabin? Why did you make that choice?

Ryan: I choose to build a cabin out of pure utility. Initially, I wanted to build a wooden yurt as I had been living in a yurt for the previous five years. The idea of living in a permanent wooden yurt appealed to me due to the circular space, completely surrounded by windows, blending beauty and utility in the structure. However, the property being remote as it is, site preparation involved felling a significant amount of pine that would be difficult to remove. As a result, I came to the conclusion to use the wood to build a traditional log cabin. I still have aspirations to build the wooden yurt, but it has been satisfying to use the wood available for the cabin.

Cabin During Construction

Beth: The security of a permanent structure matches the commitment of a life rooted in one place. Living in less permanent abodes is cheaper, simpler, adventurous, etc..., while a solid home adds the element of security to the connotation of house. We used wood from the land to the best of our abilities, and did the work ourselves. Creating a house without debt, contractors, or significant waste matches our stewardship efforts in other aspects of our life.

What was the biggest surprise once you made the move? This could either be something funny or something not-so-funny.

How much, upon leaving the property, we each want to return. It is akin to wanting to be with a family member.

What is the biggest thing you wish you had done differently right from the beginning?

Ryan: I wish I had more humour at times, not taken myself so seriously; taken time to be more celebratory, instead of constantly moving on to the next day.

Has there ever been a time since you made the move that you wished you hadn't? What happened to make you feel this way and how did you deal with these emotions or situations?

Beth: No. Both at Coösauke as well as at previous locales, there has been much security and community with close friends in the region and, more recently, my parents residing nearby.

Thus challenging periods were readily assuaged by the emotional comfort of these relationships, and the availability of physical comforts they could provide—hot water, dry space, etc.

Ryan: At times I feel that because of the lifestyle I don't allow myself enough time for personal activities. Travel, for example, is something I enjoy, but do little of because of the property—I can feel this creating resentment in myself at times.

Please share information about your property.

It's 28.34 acres, consisting of wooded hillside, river, un-maintained class VI road, remnants of 1800s era homestead, springs, sawmill, logged eight years prior, mixed hardwood forest, 1000' elevation; we must walk to arrive at the property - 0.1 mi in summer, 0.4 in winter. Originally we lived in a 16" yurt—now we live in a 16' x 18' log cabin with one room and loft above, walls of stacked logs from property, roof/floor of bought dimensional lumber.

Roofing in the Morning Mist

The total monetary cost was under $5,000 plus countless man-hours.

How much did your life change on a daily routine basis? Did you go from working in an office in a downtown setting to getting up every morning and gardening/chopping wood/ etc...?

Beth: Between the backcountry work and small-scale farming/community homestead, my life has revolved around seasonal, weather-dependent routines for some years now.

My days are dictated by weather conditions, seasonal rhythms, etc. Self-direction, motivation, and independence have been constant and necessary characteristics.

Now at Coösauke, my reality continues to be defined as such. While the tasks are similar at Coösauke, I certainly experience more freedom and independence in defining each day than I had previously.

Ryan: My work off the property never has demanded me to be clean cut or maintain a professional business appearance, so in that sense my work has been conducive to maintaining this lifestyle.

However, sometimes I do feel like I lead a double life. People will assume you live like they do, and I'm reluctant to always explain my situation, the reasons for it, etc. It can be hard to join in conversation that is based on modern entertainment, trends, etc.

I have had to make the adjustment of factoring in travel time to leave the property in the winter to adhere to agreed times. I second Beth on the influence of backcountry experiences.

What appliances and other household items did you choose not to have and why? Which ones did you choose to keep and why?

We have no power, nor running water. We have a woodstove and wood cook stove, also a ceramic water filter. The parameters of our remote location and our personal preferences keep our "appliance" list to this.

Are there any items of furniture/appliances/tools/vehicles that you use that you absolutely would not give up?

Chainsaw, bucket, broom.

What are the most useful items that you use? This could be something like a snowmobile/ATV or even something as simple as a kitchen utensil that makes your life easier/more enjoyable.

Skis, water filter, wind-up clock, garden tools, and again, chainsaw, bucket and broom.

How do you heat your home, power your home, wash clothes, cook, and obtain water?

We heat with wood, power our home with muscle, wash clothes by hand/or by friends' washing machines or the laundromat

We cook with wood, and haul water by (hand) bucket.

Cozy Interior of the Log Cabin

What do you miss from your old life? Please elaborate.

Ryan: The opportunity to watch radar, see weather in more detail.

Beth: Conveniences are convenient—hot shower, washing machine, running water—but the comfort of such easiness is short-lived. I miss the fresh air of our life more rapidly than I miss the conveniences of modernity.

What is the biggest challenge you faced after making the move?

Ryan: Keeping up on the dishes.

Beth: Explaining life to others, continually justifying decisions, choices.

How do you provide food for your family? Do you continue to shop at grocery stores/frequent farmer's markets/barter/grow your own? Please specify for both produce and meat/fish.

Beth: A combination; we have a garden that is growing with each year, as is our capacity for storage. Garden food is supplemented with local products as well as grocery store food. We eat almost exclusively vegetarian onsite, partially for philosophical reasons, partially for practicalities (no electric refrigeration). At this time, we are not raising animals (Ryan had goats in the past).

How much of your old life did you leave behind? TV, movies, shopping at the mall, internet, vacations, vehicles; anything you want to add here would be great.

Beth: We still make use of internet (off-site, for business) and vehicles. While we live quietly, seemingly apart from modern hub-bub, through jobs and social ties we are still a part of the larger world, thus we encounter the same systems and values that most people are a part of without thinking.

However, by stepping back as we have, we can be more conscious of our integration in economic/social/political/media etc... patterns and habits. That being said, life at our homestead is free of many distractions due to remoteness, lack of power, and the mountainous, rural landscape.

Ryan: I never felt like I left an old life behind; just have figured out how much or how little of the 'bull' to keep. The trail that leads to our home separates the outside world and us, figuratively and literally.

When did you know, with as much certainty as possible, that you had made the right decision?

There is so much joy in the process of our homesteading life, the other option feels miserable. Looking at it this way there is no doubt. Life keeps affirming itself as it unfolds. Friendships, associations, experiences that come along with this lifestyle have reaffirmed the certainty of this path.

If there was ever a time when you felt like you had made the wrong decision, when was it and why did you feel that way?

Not seriously. Doubt is never eliminated, but the questions around major life decisions are not akin to an erroneous course. If you let doubt overtake you, you'll never develop the confidence to do anything.

Did your circle of friends change? Did you lose friends over this change in your lives, gain new ones?

Yes, they got crazier!

Ryan: Yes I have lost some friends from lack of communication. But I wouldn't attribute it to homesteading.

Beth: Friends have questioned what I've done, not understood what I'm pursuing, but close friends have either remained, or come back. I think in some way my surety in choosing something and doing something whole-heartedly has brought me greater friendships, and strengthened existing ones. My pursuit of something real, somehow translates to the way in which I can be with people—this is sensed, and seems to reciprocate very real, deep friendships.

What are the greatest rewards you have experienced in your life because of your decision to change your lifestyle?

Beth: I find much joy and comfort in a lifestyle that reaffirms my ideals. It is much easier to maintain a sense of grounded-ness, maintain a center, stability. The distractions and values of the "real world" seem plastic and glossy by comparison, and therefore have less bearing on my judgement and decisions. There is power in independence and the confidence to be one's own compass.

My life is my own.

Ryan: So far the greatest rewards have been the intimacy with the land that I share, and the people who have stuck around throughout the endeavour. I appreciate living in one place: one bio-region to learn and observe the seasonal changes, cycles, and particulars that one learns from living deliberately and being at the will of the landscape and weather.

Homesteading has reaffirmed my confidence and also has given me a different reference point in which I live my life.

What are the biggest challenges you have faced?

Beth: Physically, building the cabin has certainly been a challenge to our skills, but not so great as to obscure a pleasure in the construction (and learning) process. Mentally, there have been cold nights due to lack of insulation or lack of heat source (in previous living situations) where I had to laugh at myself to keep from feeling crazy. I suppose the real challenge, though, is simply the process of growing and being in the world, and making choices with confidence and compassion.

Ryan: The biggest challenge to me is how to live a balance between the homestead and the world "at-large." How much of my passion for other work is enough as it takes me off the property. The challenge is truly of a mental nature, as most of life is.

Did you experience any issues with building codes/municipal laws that hindered your set-up in regards to building/land use/septic or other permits?

Ryan: Yes. First it took two years to get an address because I needed a 911 number. I could not get a 911 number because the town selectman chose not to accept and acknowledge the yurt as a habitable structure (which is not actually needed to have a 911 number). Using this argument it took two years to petition for a number.

For a while I had mail sent to our road without a number until the local postmaster demanded I had a number. So I took it upon myself to give the property the number of 7; this worked for a while, until the postmaster realized it wasn't the actual 911 number (he is friends with the selectman). I inquired about general delivery but the postmaster again said that would not be allowed and I would have to get a PO Box—which I quickly refused since the mail truck passes my road daily.

So I continued to get my mail in the previous residence I held in another town. .

It wasn't until I was granted a building permit that I was given a 911 number and finally had mail delivered to my actual address.

But in order to get a building permit, (since the property lies on a class VI un-maintained town road) I had to apply for and sign a road release granting the town "harmless" of any duties in the upkeep of the road which deferred it to us.

Overall, the experience of building and living an alternative lifestyle within the confines of conventional culture can be difficult for officials to deal with as these situations seem to fall within a lot of "grey areas" of law, codes, etc.

If there were three pieces of advice that you would give someone considering making this lifestyle change, what would they be?

Beth: 1) Don't do this to find yourself. Know yourself, then act to bring yourself, thoughts, and actions into agreement.

2) Maintain perspective—I often remind myself that along the geologic timeline we are but a blip; therefore humility and comfort with one's own vulnerability is crucial. Laughter is essential.

3) You don't have to do everything at once.

Ryan: 1) Don't take yourself too seriously; have humour.

2) Take time for yourself and the things you enjoy and remember your doing this to have more opportunity for these things.

3) Don't isolate yourself—involve family, friends, and community.

Do you feel that you have gained much more in your life than you gave up? Please explain.

Beth: Yes. My life is my own.

Ryan: I share the same perspective as Beth in that I didn't give up anything, but was discriminating as to what to accept and reject in life (what is useful and what is not).

Have you started any new hobbies since you made the move, and if so, how did you discover your newfound interest(s)?

Beth: I have made a minor attempt to learn the mandolin...I would say overall that I have been able to dedicate time to existing endeavours that had previously been pushed to the sidelines. For me, these primarily include writing and hiking.

Ryan: Yes, initially through the mountains and then through my own self-inquiry into the subject of existence, I have become a student of Buddhism and am active in the local Shambhala Buddhist community.

I have found the act of homesteading, backcountry pursuits, and community involvement very conducive to leading a contemplative life, spiritual, but not necessarily religious.

By being so intimately connected with the phenomenal world,
the very simple acts that we do daily
become rituals in many ways,
just as meaningful as religious ritual.

How did you make a living prior to your move and what do you do now?

Beth: Post-college, I maintained myself on unusual jobs that prepared me—sometimes unintentionally—for the homesteading life. I spent five years working in various capacities in the White Mountains of NH, being a caretaker, steward, Sherpa, educator, and search and rescue contact. I then spent four years living and working at a permaculture farm/educational homestead/community, also in NH. There I performed a variety of tasks, including garden management, animal husbandry, ox-powered forestry, hospitality, cooking/preservation, grant writing and communications, administration, accounting, and more.

These jobs paid minimally, but included room and board, significantly expanded my skills, and allowed for almost 100% savings so long as personal expenses were at a minimum. I was able to align making a life and making a living fairly closely.

Now living at Coösauke, I work as a writer/editor, as well as performing garden design/property management services as commissioned. My philosophy, to the best of my ability, is to use my physical energy for our property, and use my intellectual energy to earn a living. I therefore engage in grant writing services, freelance articles, press content, blog articles, and editing services, all of which I am able to complete from a computer (off-site).

Trained in permaculture and organic methods, I also offer annual/perennial/herbal/medicinal/ornamental garden design and management, as well as consultations for developing and implementing edible landscapes. This coincides well with Ryan's forestry/land management work, allowing us to offer landowners within the New England region a complete range of property management services.

You can reach Bethann Weick, to contract design work or written pieces at:

b.a.weick@gmail.com

You can also follow their adventures at Coösauke via Mother Earth News' Happy Homesteader blog (under the Happy Homesteader icon) at:

http://www.motherearthnews.com

Bethann also writes for Northcountry News:

http://www.northcountrynewsnh.com/

Ryan: For the past eight years I have served as the trails foreman for the White Mountain National Forest as well as working part-time for a consulting forester, mountain caretaker, and other mountain-related positions. More recently I have become more of an individual resource working independently in the fields of forestry, land management, and trail work.

It is my prerogative to continue this and have more flexibility in my schedule and variety in my work. I will be applying for a forester's license in the state of New Hampshire and work with landowners balancing timber resource interests, habitat, and recreational resources. Along with that, I continue to work in the professional field of trail work within public and private lands.

I look forward to collaborating with Beth in these fields, as I become more of an independent contractor. I call my contracting business Wildland Services encompassing many of my passions from natural habitat interpretation, forestry, trails consultation and construction, to traditional tools skills training.

Are there any final thoughts you would like to share with our readers?

For us, homesteading is largely about both change and deliberation. Even since first sharing the previous descriptions of our lifestyle, much has changed. Structures, details of the landscape, seasons, resources, gardens—these physical changes have slowly grown and morphed as days passed into weeks passed into months. Too, plans have taken shape, dreams have developed, new designs, imaginings, habits have emerged, altered, evolved. The act of living, rooted, on one piece of land engaged in work dedicated to a simple abundance offers remarkable steadiness and permanence; yet this exists simultaneous to the constant of change. Creativity, flexibility, humor, consideration, reflection, and freshness are engendered by the pervasiveness of change on a daily level.

Accepting such change as a perpetual companion seems, to us, to also promote bravery, confidence, laughter, and openness. Change is not a source of fear or anxiety, but an opportunity to re-enter each moment. In this way, homesteading is also about being deliberate. It is about exercising curiosity and inquisitiveness as we negotiate choices and decisions. Ryan likes to paraphrase a Shambhala chant to highlight this: we strive to ride the moment, rather than the moment riding us. The homesteading lifestyle, for us, is about living consciously and enjoying the act of being fully alive.

✳✳✳

Conclusion

I'd like to thank all of our contributors, for their time, for their willingness to share, for their openness about their lives and experiences, for their advice, and for being such an inspiration to those like Mike and I, and our readers, who are preparing for *A Way of Life Less Common*.

Each of our contributors chose to share their stories with us without compensation, which says a lot about the type of people they are.

If you choose to visit their websites, read their blogs, or contact them (they have much more to share than what could be contained in this book) please let them know you found them in *A Way of Life Less Common*. Share your appreciation for their stories and insights, so they know how valuable their contributions to this book really were.

As you've learned from reading their interviews, our contributors come from all walks of life, with diverse backgrounds and different life paths—but all found their way to accomplish what many only ever dream of doing. Let them be an inspiration to you—anything in life is possible if you set your mind to it and work toward your goals.

We will share with you as we embark on this exciting journey, and we will update out progress on our upcoming blog.

Mike will also be sharing his amazing recipes on our Cottage Country Cook blog (cottagecountrycook.com), also being designed at the moment.

Although this is the conclusion to this book, it is only the beginning chapter of our lives and the exciting books we will be releasing in the future.

Thank you for reading this book and we hope you will visit our website often for new releases in this series.

Christine Dixon & Mike Carter

Coming Soon
A Way of Life
Less Common
Modern Day Pioneers
Volume Two

If you would like to share your experiences living in the bush, going off-grid, or homesteading, please contact us for more information on being interviewed and included in our next volume.

We are also preparing new titles in this series, so visit us often. You may have the next great story to share. Visit CottageCountryPress.com and click on our submission page. We're working on several exciting titles!

We also invite you to share in our experiences as we prepare to embark on this journey ourselves.

Christine Dixon & Mike Carter
www.CottageCountryPress.com
vangoach@bmts.com